# Th[illegible]
# £1,0[illegible]
# Share Punter



by

**Michael Walters**

First published February 2000 by Laddingford Books



ISBN-0-9537973-0-9

Printed by Identity, Unit 25, Branbridges Industrial Estate, East Peckham, Kent TN12 5HF

# The £1,000 Share Punter

by

Michael Walters

Laddingford Books

# CONTENTS

# WARNING

Do not buy this book unless you have money you can afford to lose. Buying and selling shares is an extremely dangerous business. Unless you are lucky, you will lose money on some of the shares you buy. You might lose money on every one, and could end up losing every penny of your stake money.

This is not a conventional, fuddy-duddy book about investing. It is designed to help those who understand that all share trading is a form of gambling, and many gamblers end up losers.

Hopefully, however, this is not a book for losers. Playing the stock market is the greatest game I know. It can be enormous fun. And it can be highly rewarding. You may get lucky and land one big win. Or you may get smart, and end up winning more than you lose because you have some idea of what you are doing.

These days, many of us can find £1,000 or £2,000 to play with, if we really want to. Leaving it in the bank or building society is hardly worthwhile. Punting on the stock market might just make a difference. Hit it right, and £1,000 or £2,000 could become £10,000, maybe more, if you are smart enough or lucky enough. And the internet has brought an information revolution. For the first time, private investors have the opportunity of finding out what is happening, as it happens.

This book is for those who are prepared to be just a little bit brave, gambling with the kind of money they would not miss too much. The bull market will not last forever. While it is running, the small punters should be out there, having fun. A few might just do well enough to change their lives for the richer. That is why so many have suddenly discovered the stock market – the greatest Millennium game in town.

Go for it – but be prepared to lose.

Michael Walters

# Introduction

On the morning of Saturday, October 9, 1999, I drove from my home in Kent to meet a group of investors who followed the bulletin board on the Moneyworld internet financial advice site. Fifty or sixty of them had scrambled out of cyberspace to meet in the flesh and to swap ideas. They invited me to talk about penny shares. Inevitably, they wanted a tip or two.

Ill-prepared, and in a rush as usual, I suggested that a little company called eVestment might be worth backing. I liked and knew the management. They had recently re-named the company and re-directed it, and it had embarked on a new life as an internet incubator fund. It was 3 1/2p, and looked as if it might benefit from the growing fashion for internet investments.

Almost immediately after that meeting, I went to America for a fortnight. On my return, eVestment was 6 1/2p. I noticed there had been chat on the internet bulletin boards, some of it suggesting I had tipped it. I did try to tip eVestment in my Daily Mail Saturday Investment Extra column a little later, but it never appeared. Half of the column was scrapped at short notice to make way for something else in the paper. So I never actually recommended eVestment in the Mail, even when I tipped a bunch of internet stocks on October 30, though I did mention it elsewhere.

My timing was lucky. In the first week of November, small internet stocks suddenly caught fire. Private investors began throwing money into incubator funds and almost anything else with dot com in the name. Prices began to soar. Two or three weeks later, most national newspaper pundits switched on the auto pilot, and began to predict doom and disaster for them. The usual City suspects were corralled, and joined the chorus. It would all end in tears, we were assured.

By December, net stocks were flying. eVestment topped 48p fuelled by inaccurate rumours of alliances ahead. In fact, the company announced a fund-raising at 8p a share, bringing in more board-room muscle with powerful new shareholders in the background. The shares dipped to 38p, then 32p, touched 22p, then bounced above 30p again.

The details do not matter. It had been a brilliant run for the Moneyworld boys and girls who met in Walsall. Several of them had bought eVestment at under 4p. At one point, they had multiplied their money twelve-fold in seven or eight weeks. Ponder that. If they had put £1,000 into eVestment in the middle of October, they would have had £12,000 at the peak early in December. Even at Christmas, with the price back to 32p, they would have seen their £1,000 multiply to £8,000. You can make big money fast – and they did. I know some of them actually pocketed fat profits, selling before Christmas.

Forgive me if this sounds as if I am patting myself on my back. Of course I am. More to the point, though, is that this is an example from real life, not some dry, theoretical exercise. I got lucky, and so did the MoneyWorld investors (I should say that I also tipped them two other penny stocks which did not do nearly so well, Minmet and Gladstone. At one point in the eight weeks, Minmet was up about 50pc, while Gladstone doubled). But the Walsall Moneyworld crew certainly discovered, in real life, that with a little luck, a little knowledge, and nerve enough to take a gamble, punting in shares can make a great deal of difference – and fast.

Do not misunderstand. The eVestment tip was a fluke, part of an unprecedented internet share explosion. In almost forty years of writing about investment, I cannot recall anything quite like it. The only thing to come close was the great Australian mining share boom in the sixties, when hundreds of thousands of small punters hung on every word from the late Charles Lloyd, City Editor of the Sun. A few made fortunes overnight. Many more lost the lot when the bubble burst.

But eVestment was not the only share to soar in that couple of months before Christmas 1999. Others rocketed – I tipped some of them. On Christmas Eve 1999, two new issues – JellyWorks and Internet Indirect – had gone from 5p on flotation to top 100p and 90p respectively in a few days.

The internet share explosion might end in tears. There certainly will be heavy losers at some stage. Never mind. So long as you are not one of them, it does not matter to you. And if you can learn to ignore the standard City nonsense about holding for the long term, it need not be you. Shares are simply pieces of paper which people buy and sell on the stock market. Sometimes the price goes up, sometimes down. The whole point of the game is to buy when the price is down, and to sell when it goes up - nothing more.

Do not let the standard City noise about long-term investment, fundamental value, accounting issues, spreading the risk, and so on, distract you. If such things appear really important to you, do not buy this book. It does address them, but with pretty scant reverence. There are plenty of perfectly good books on investment theory around.

This book is not about investment theory – it is unashamedly about helping private investors to make money. You do not need a fortune to play the stock market – £1,000 or so will do. With a little luck, and perhaps a little help from this book, you might manage to make it into £2,000. Or £3,000… maybe even more. And have fun along the way.

It can be done. I know. Through the years, many small investors have contacted me, telling me how they started with a few thousand and have multiplied it to £10,000 or more. Through 1999, I am delighted to report, their numbers have risen sharply. Some have been helped by my tips, some have followed other successful tipsters in the press or in newsletters. Yet more have been finding ideas of their own, following postings on internet bulletin boards, swapping ideas with like-minded share punters.

I also know it can be done because I am a small share punter myself. I use the word "punter" quite deliberately. It conveys an appropriate air of speculation. For more than thirty years, I have played the market in a relatively small way – small because I have not had much money. Twice I have made a pretty useful killing, and twice lost or spent most of it. At the time of writing, I am doing quite nicely. I hope to hang on to it this time.

It is important that readers of this book know I play the market. It means that I have some idea of how it really works, and do not draw simply on theory. It also means that I may sometimes own the shares I write about, though my dealings are covered by pretty strict rules which put me at a disadvantage to readers. I should also point out that I left the Daily Mail in October 1998 after 21 years to work for Square Mile Communications, a financial public relations company. This has given me valuable insight into investment from another angle, and more freedom to visit companies. But it does present another potential conflict of interest everyone should keep in mind – sometimes I do write about companies which are clients of Square Mile.

There is a revolution going on among private investors. They have tossed aside the boring old City investment stereotypes, and are out there in the market, empowered by the internet, having fun, and making money while the opportunity lasts. Long may they prosper.

Michael Walters. January 2000.

# ONE

## *GETTING DOWN TO BASICS*

Year in, year out, they grind away. Pick up the City pages of the national newspapers, and the chances are that in any month of any year from 1994 onward, there will be some pundit predicting a stock market collapse.

Yet as we entered the New Millennium, stock markets in London and New York were pushing on to new highs. Stockbroking offices were overwhelmed with orders from private investors eager to take advantage of soaring prices of internet-related shares. Business had multiplied five-fold, ten-fold, as more and more people fretted about the tiny returns available from leaving money in the bank, and turned to the stock market in the hope of seeing a more spectacular return on their money.

Still the columns appeared, often quietly sneering at small investors. Tired old clichés were re-cycled endlessly. Time and again, there was some variation on the old maxim that the time to sell was when taxi-drivers started talking about share tips. Or some such condescending nonsense, gently implying that the writer was above such things, and understood that only real players could know about share trading. The instant the masses got involved, it was time for the proper professionals to leave.

This is arrogant, unthinking rubbish. By the time you read this, the market may have taken a tumble. The fun might be over for a while. Share prices might have crashed, and private investors may be nursing their losses. On the other hand, perhaps all is still well. Who can guess? One thing is certain – if and when there is a crash, the biggest losers will be the professionals, the so-called experts. They are the boys with big money in the market. And they and their employers are the ones who will really hurt if there is a crash.

The pundits will be preaching a different lesson by then, of course. At that point, everyone will be counselling patience, suggesting that it is too late to sell, hammering away that the market always recovers, that the long term trend is always up.

So it has been – and so it almost certainly will be. Be careful, though. The truth is that none of us actually knows. The "experts" who predict a crash have no clearer idea than you or I. They are guessing. Maybe you are smart enough to see the future with 20-20 vision. If so, you have no need of this book.

Equally, none of us can predict a rising market with any real degree of confidence. We are all guessing, all of the time. Sometimes, though, you can shade the odds in your favour, improve the chances of getting it right, by spending time trying to understand more of how things work. This book is an effort at trying to help the private investor along that route. Whatever happens, over the next few years more and more private investors are likely to discover the stock market, and will play the game. I hope you will join them. And I hope you will understand that "investment" is just another way of talking about gambling on the stock market, long term, short term, or whatever.

There are many books which deal with how much you should save, whether it should be in an Individual Savings Account, in an investment trust or a unit trust, the complications of accounts, discounted cash flow, accelerated depreciation, fundamental values. I have written some of them – "How To Make A Killing In The Share Jungle", and "How to Make A Killing In Penny Shares" are the best-known. If you have read them and feel this book covers too much of the same ground, I am sorry. This pays less attention to such matters, and more to the day-to-day business of what counts in a share market where the short-term has become more important then ever. If too much of it is too familiar, I apologise.

This is a pretty personal book, deliberately written in informal style, hopefully rather like a chat with friends. It rambles around, and makes the same points over and again. They are the only ones I know. If they work, I stick with them. To me, they are crucial. For better or worse, they colour my whole approach to shares and the stock market. They are based on the lessons which have been hammered home through the years, making and losing money as a small investor, learning the share market the hard way. Sorry if they seem trite and obvious – but you forget them at your peril.

## THE ESSENTIAL RULES

### NEVER USE MORE THAN YOU CAN AFFORD TO LOSE

Almost everyone will tell you this, if they remember. It is absolute common sense. You must never be tempted to risk more than you can afford to lose, no matter how sure you are that you have found a winner. And yet... a few of my pals have come a cropper through the years. I came pretty close once. We all get greedy. Where £100 profit used to seem brilliant, after a while, it does not seem so large. Why not try for £500? And so on.

It becomes especially dangerous when you have made a few profits. Suddenly you begin to think this share game is not so tricky, after all. If only you had put £2,000 on that winner instead of £1,000, think of what you would have made. Twice as much. Now you are getting to know more about it – watching the chat on the internet bulletin boards, perhaps – you can afford to be a little braver, surely ?

Beware. The most dangerous stage of the share game is when you have had a little success, and get cocky. You will. It is human nature. Guard against it. The market can change dramatically in an instant.

In 1974, when National Westminster Bank shares were selling for a few pence and the chairman effectively issued a statement to the Stock Exchange denying the bank was going bust, it seemed like the end of the stock market world. Everything, good or bad, had slumped. Even the best-known names looked almost worthless. If you had to sell then, you would have lost almost all of your money.

In October 1987, the market crashed by 25pc in two days. Some shares halved, in big companies as well as small. Just because that did not happen yesterday, do not think it cannot happen again. It could. You may get little warning. It still happens regularly to individual shares. eVestment, the soaraway share in my introduction, leapt twelve-fold in eight weeks. Yet at one stage, it fell from the 48p peak to 22p in a few days. There were people piling in, paying more than 48p. Within hours they were bemoaning their lot on internet bulletin boards, debating whether to hold or sell after they had lost half of their money. Those, perhaps, were the lucky ones. They could afford to pay. There will have been others who had bought more shares than they could afford, and who were forced to sell at half price, whether they liked it or not. Alongside the happy punters who made a quick killing in eVestment, there were some casualties. Totally exterminated share punters.

## *THERE IS NO SUCH THING AS A SURE THING*

You know that. You know that wherever you look, at the race track, the Cup Final, the tip sheet, there is no sure thing.

That applies with a vengeance to investment. Do not be tempted to use more than you can afford to lose. Someone knows more than you do, understands what is going on, and has been tipped off about higher profits, or a takeover bid. If your informant really does know, the chances are that they are passing on inside information, confidential stuff which it is illegal to pass on or to use. Defining inside information can be a touch tricky, but you are much more likely to get caught than some City slicker who has the real inside information. Prosecutions have been few and far between, but most of those convicted have been small investors. The Stock Exchange has a system which can track who is behind almost any share deal – where it falls down is in establishing the motive for that deal. The City boys can duck and dive in a way you could never match. They might escape, but you probably will not.

If you are not acting on inside information, your sure thing is even more likely to go wrong. You can try to check, of course, and form a pretty shrewd opinion. That is essential to successful investing. But there is nothing so sure that you should risk too much on it. Think about Marks & Spencer, revered by unthinking City Editors, tipped time and again. In 1997, they loved it at 665p. Late in 1999, they were praying someone would bid for it at 250p.

## *DO NOT BELIEVE A WORD THEY SAY*

A touch over-emphatic, perhaps, this one. It might be better to emphasise merely that you should think for yourself.

It has always amused me to hear people say that they do not believe a word they read in the papers. Then they talk about something they have read somewhere. Fair enough. We all gather what we can, any way we can. We can all benefit from another opinion, and all learn from each other. But it is unwise to take anything in the share game on trust. As one who knows how they work, I do have sympathy for those who question newspaper stories. They are invariably gathered in great haste and confusion, and often filtered through a collection of half-truths. Please, though, adopt a similarly sceptical approach to other sources. None of them are perfect.

There is no tipster who does not make mistakes (I know, I know), no pundit who does not get it wildly wrong at times. Most of us understand that. But it is easier to be deceived by the so-called professionals. When you read the chairman's statement, is he always right? Does he always tell the whole story? And the auditors? How many companies which have been given a clean bill of health by some top-flight, overpaid accountancy firm, then gone bust a few months later? That applies to almost every company which goes bust. How can it be that Geoffrey Robinson and TransTec were suddenly seen to be in such a state when not a word appeared in the last accounts about the massive damages claim from Ford?

And how many stockbrokers have issued long, detailed, immensely learned reports on a public company, explaining exactly why you should buy the shares, only to see them slump soon after?

It is easy to mock, and right to do so from time to time. Most people do their best to get it right. But we all make honest mistakes. And some make a few downright dishonest errors, too. So when you read or hear anything, do not simply accept it as correct. Ask yourself if it really makes sense, if it is something you can trust completely. The answer, you may find, is often somewhere in between. Always question, always try to check, always make up your own mind. You will be risking your own money.

## *ONLY DO WHAT YOU CAN UNDERSTAND*

It is extraordinary how well some City folk manage to project an air of effortless superiority. There is a mystique about money-making which lingers on. Many of the processes are extremely complex, and beyond the wit of most of us. And that is where they should stay.

Should anyone try to persuade you to put money into a scheme you do not understand, do not do it. This is not to say that you should not buy a biotechnology share, or an internet play because you do not really understand what the company does. Few of us do. The best we can do is make a partly-informed guess (more on that later).

But if someone shows you a document, explains what it means, and suggests this is good reason for you to part with your money, insist on a full explanation of why it is so good. Be sure you follow the reasoning. Sometimes if things are obscure, they are meant to be that way. Documents are carefully designed to disclose just what suits the parties concerned. If the process does not make sense to you, do not be intimidated. Never hesitate to ask the obvious question, the one which might seem to betray your ignorance. What puzzles you might just be designed to deceive.

In any event, if you invest without fully understanding something which has been troubling you, yours is the money you will lose if it goes wrong. Who will feel foolish then?

## *GREED IS GOOD – IF IT IS ON YOUR SIDE*

Though there were some who huffed and puffed over the Gordon Gekko character in the film "Wall Street", and deplored his "Greed is good" speech, it makes some sense. There is no point in playing the stock market if you are offended by greed and the notion of making money. That is what the game is about.

What you want is a greedy entrepreneur who is going to make money for himself, and who will make money for you in the process. No point in buying shares in a company whose board is content with life, happy to sit back and let events take their course. What you want is someone who wants to make things happen, and in the process will make things happen for you. Just try to satisfy yourself that his greed will not be satisfied at your expense, and that the deals he proposes do not enrich him without making money for you, too.

No-one is in the share game for altruistic motives. Everyone has an angle. They are there because they want to make money somehow. Keep that in mind, and try to see that the angle which counts is the one which suits your game.

## *LISTEN TO WHAT THE MARKET IS TELLING YOU*

When you think about it, you appreciate why this old market maxim makes sense. Very broadly, the course of share prices is determined by the weight of money. The more money being spent on buying shares, the higher they rise. The more cash being taken out by sellers, the further they fall.

Look behind that, and question why someone is buying, or selling. In reality, you can never really know. There could always be people buying or selling for reasons totally unrelated to the merits of the share itself – they might need the cash to buy a house, or could be selling to meet death duties, or a tax bill. In many cases, though, the buyer or seller may feel they know something about the merits of the underlying company. Sometimes they will have inside information. At other times, someone will have done some research into the industry, and be ahead of the herd in discovering factors which will influence the success of the business.

Whatever the truth, if a share starts rising or falling, it rarely does so for long without good reason. What the price is telling you is that someone may know more than you do, and is acting upon it. So pay attention when a share starts to rise for no apparent reason. The buyers may know something good. And – especially – take heed if the price should begin to fall. Someone who really knows something may be selling.

The information the market tells you through the price movement is not infallible. But you ignore it at your risk.

## *CUT YOUR LOSSES, AND RUN YOUR PROFITS*

Once you have actually bought a share – any share – this is the most important rule of all. And it is the one most people ignore most frequently.

Unlike other forms of gambling, share trading can give you a second, third, or fourth chance. Maybe more. If you get it wrong, and pick a loser, you can sell and retrieve part of your stake before it is all lost. You can use it to play again, giving yourself the chance of being right second time. Or third time even. Though the market is becoming more volatile, it is relatively rare for shares to become worthless overnight. In most cases, they start drifting lower, and stock market reports often indicate that there are worries about something or other.

That is when the sensible investor will sell. The market is telling everyone, through the falling price, that something might be wrong. If you have bought a share and the price is down by, say, 20pc, the chances are that you have made a mistake. Recognise it, sell, and use what you have left to play again.

Cutting your losses quickly is almost more important than picking a winner. So long as you do not actually lose your stake money, you can always change your mind, sell, and try again. Once that stake money is gone, you are out of the game. So if you see your share start to fall, admit you might have made a mistake, and move on to something else.

If you have been smart or lucky enough to find a winner, stay with it while it rises. Do not sell until it starts to reverse. It is not easy to find a winner. When you have one, stick with it, make the most of it. The market almost always overdoes things, pushing troubled shares too low, and boosting winners too high.

Sadly, the majority of punters appear only too keen to sell winners in order to stick with losers, hoping something will turn up. It makes no sense. It may be easy to understand – none of us likes admitting we were wrong – but you should try to take the emotion out of share buying and especially out of selling. No matter how attached to it you become, no share ever realises that you love it. No share ever feels it needs to return your patience and your love. It will dump you, along with all of the other losers.

## *LIMIT THE DOWNSIDE*

For more than thirty years, I have advocated a stop loss system. Put simply, when a share falls by a certain percentage, say 20pc, sell it regardless. If you have a winner, raise the stop loss price behind the actual share price. And when it falls, say 20pc, from the peak, take your profits and sell. That way, though you never get out at the top, you do preserve some profits.

Crucially, such a system helps reduce the risk in investing. If you have determined that you will sell a share should it show a loss of 20pc, you have reduced the risk of buying that share. You can almost determine how much loss you are willing to stand, if things should go wrong. Set the stop loss at 10pc, 20pc, 30pc – even 50pc – and you have reduced the chance of total loss. The system is not infallible. Sometimes prices slump too fast for you to sell on the way down. But more often than not, it works.

Cutting losses quickly is part of the discipline of limiting the downside. None of us buys a share without dreaming of the gains we might make. The upside encourages us to buy. But trying to measure the downside is an essential part of the game. Before you buy, try to judge what could go wrong, where the weaknesses may be in your strategy. Inevitably, there will be dangers. Assess them as objectively as you can. Do not take on 50/50 bets. If you are aware that your choice could carry significant risks, only play if you can be reasonably sure that the potential gains are correspondingly greater. If the risks really are that heavy, do not be tempted. Walk away.

For as long as I can remember, my first instinct in assessing any possible investment has been to calculate what could go wrong. Perhaps that comes from years as a financial journalist – you roll up for a press conference, or a meeting with the chief executive, aware that everyone is trying to project the brightest possible image – so you automatically look for the snags, the things they are not telling you. As an investor, it is not a bad approach. Companies rarely rush to tell anyone the bad news. When they have problems, they seek to play them down.

Whatever you look at, try to imagine what would happen if things went wrong, what the shares might be worth if the exciting new venture did not take off, or the competition cut in with something bigger. You could easily talk yourself out of buying anything at all if you overplay the doom and gloom. But do not forget it. It really helps to focus your mind.

# TWO

## *WHO CARES ABOUT PROFITS?*

Go back to the beginning. Strip the mystique away, the acres of print about the economy, management philosophies, corporate governance, and all of that stuff, and ponder why you are bothering about buying shares.

No matter what, you are buying shares to make money, nothing else. Be sure about this. It does not really matter to you whether British Telecommunications is a great British company, or a greedy near-monopolist choking the growth of the internet by over-charging and under-investing. Or whether Tesco is strangling the High Street. Or Sir Alan Sugar is a warm, cuddly character, or a shrewd money-maker.

However you may feel about such things, it makes no great difference to you as a share trader. All you want to know is whether the shares are likely to go up or down. BT shares did brilliantly in 1999, Marks & Spencer slumped, and Sugar's Amstrad soared. That is what matters most to you, the share punter. Inevitably, your more general opinions will exert some influence on investment choices, but you should try to filter them out. Remember – shares are pieces of paper. Some go up, some go down.

There is a mass of ambient noise around share trading, much of it routinely intended to mislead. The City establishment is very big on long-term investment. Buy, put it away, and wake up in twenty years – it should be better then.

I deplore this attitude, and the patronising air which supports it. It smacks of the old "we know best" attitude which pervades parts of the City. No need to bother your head with stuff like buying and selling shares, old chap. Let us take care of it for you. We understand it.

Shares do go up over the long term. Surveys galore suggest that the indices which measure share price performance almost always rise over any five year period. And they do fare better than money left in the building society.

This may be fine for pension fund money, for your basic savings. But if you are reading this book, you do not want to bother with such stuff. You want something more dynamic. You are playing with money you can afford to lose, and nursing the dream that you might just make it into something really worthwhile. You will rarely do that by leaving it with the City to look after. A 10pc gain over the year is counted excellent by long term City standards. A gain of 10pc on your £1,000 is £100 – hardly life-changing. Even 20pc makes little difference.

The long term, too, covers a mass of City sins. Indolence – dump the cash into a solid portfolio of well-known shares, and though you reap annual management fees, you do not actually have to do anything to earn them. Ignorance – everyone understands the big companies evolve slowly and are well-researched by City stockbrokers, so they spring few surprises, and it is not worth the trouble of really understanding how they work. Errors – spread the money around among enough big names, and it does not matter if one goes badly wrong because it will not make that much difference to the whole, and no-one will really notice. And so on.

There is also another important element in the unfailing flow of advice to hold on for the longer term – the boys do not want you to sell. Look at the structure of big investment management groups. They buy big chunks of shares in the larger companies, and sit with them for years on end, allocating small portions to a series of different investment funds they run. Though there are individual variations, by and large, most houses have a common investment policy. If they like one share, they buy it for all of their funds.

That makes sense. But it makes it more difficult for them to sell. If the house view changes, which funds sell first ? If one sells, it might undermine the value of the other funds held in the same investment house. If they sell all of the holding at once, clearing it out of all funds together, there would be too many shares to sell easily at the market price. Knowledge that a particular house was a seller would push the price down against them. And against the other houses who hold the stock – they all tend to be sheep, and many hold more or less the same stocks.

They have to sell when shares are rising, because that is the only time they can easily find buyers. If one big seller wants out, someone has to buy the stock. So the pressure to sell when the market is rising builds in a degree of underperformance. Or simply ensures that the boys do not sell. They sit tight, and hope for the best.

The last thing they want is to see small investors pumping shares out. Because the big boys tend to be long term holders, great chunks of many companies never change hands. The price is effectively determined by the 10pc, 20pc, or 30pc held by more active operators. Some of them are big funds, but many are smaller traders. So the individual investor tends to exert a disproportionate influence on price movements. It is easy to overstate it, but to a degree, short term traders, often a mass of smaller investors, help dictate the price. You are not going to swing markets with your £1,000 deals – but if enough private punters move the same way, then watch 'em go.

There are many companies with a market value of £250m or more where the price will move by 5pc if a seller comes in to shift £50,000 of stock on a bad day. That £50,000 sale could wipe £12.5m off the market value of the company. Or a £50,000 buy, of course, could raise it by £12.5m. The market capitalisation of companies under £100m or so can swing quite sharply if a couple of £10,000 orders come in close together on a quiet day.

So pay no mind to City talk about the virtues of long term investment. It is not intended to help you, but is pure City self-interest speaking. And all that really matters to the £1,000 share punter is making as large a profit as quickly as possible, not boring for Britain with some plank of the establishment.

## *Short Term Trading*

It all comes wrapped up in a vague notion that somehow long term investing is virtuous, and short term trading is rather vulgar, nasty stuff which proper City chaps frown on. That, too, is part of the great City confidence trick. In reality, some of the greediest, craftiest share trading spivs work for the best-known names, the most outwardly respectable houses. They do it more elegantly than most, but they do it. Never imagine that it was just in the Middle Ages that the robber barons built the fortunes which still sustain aristocratic pretensions in the 21st Century. They may not be raping, but they are still quietly plundering and pillaging all over the Square Mile. Look at some of the fees disclosed in company deal documents. Watch how shares in takeover targets almost always rise ahead of bid announcements. No-one gets prosecuted, because at the highest level they know how to do it better.

Never, for one instant, be deterred from making and taking a quick profit by a vague feeling that it is not quite the done thing. Do it. Take it. The boys in the business never hesitate.

### *Concentrating your efforts*

Another great establishment mantra drones that you must spread your risks. Rubbish. If you are a small share punter you simply cannot afford to do it. Accept that you are gambling, and might have a decent spread of financial risk elsewhere. When you are punting the market, there is nothing wrong in concentrating your efforts. Goodness knows it is hard enough to find a flyer. When you have one, you want to make the most of it.

If you have £1,000, you really do need to play with one share, at the most two. And £2,000 should be spread over just one or two shares. Perhaps if you get to £5,000, then you might go up to two or three. If you get to £10,000, maybe four would be right. Put simply, if you have a stock with a 50pc gain, you would make £250 if you are playing with £1,000, but it is split between two shares. If the full £1,000 is in one stock, you have a £500 gain. And so on. If you are going to gamble, go for it wholeheartedly.

Spreading your risk at this level only means incurring extra dealing costs, and diluting the impact of a winner. It may almost be better to think about pyramiding – buying more once you have a winner which is beginning to move.

Jim Slater might shudder to think I was pinching his idea and applying it this way, but if you get a chance to read his valuable book "The Zulu Principle", you will find why he picked that title. His wife read a piece about the Zulus, and took an interest. If she then began reading all she could about them, she would soon have become an expert compared to most of us. Focussing on a narrow subject might put you ahead of the crowd. Concentrating on learning about a few small shares might help you pick the best of them. You only have so much time and so much capital. Focus. Use it wisely. No point in trying to compete against the City in knowing about the top 250 companies. You will never beat them at that, and because so much is known about them, the chances of a pleasant surprise are modest – though some will rise sharply.

### *Value Investing*

Then we come to an altogether trickier area – the business of value investing and company fundamentals. This, too, comes with a variety of moral and intellectual baggage. It is easy to see why. The old work ethic weighs in vaguely. It says that if you are going to make money in the share market, you should have to graft for it. You should be required to discover what your intended investment company really does, and you should understand that the best companies are those which make lots of money and are stuffed full of big fat assets just in case things go wrong.

Whoops. Suddenly it sounds as if this share game is about to get very complicated. Any proper player would have to master all sorts of accounting and analytical skills to work a way through that little lot. Or would they?

Do not be put off. There is nothing which says you should not just buy shares blind, knowing only the name, and hoping for the best. You might be lucky. A lucky investor might beat a skilled one any time – but not with any consistency.

You are never going to learn enough to feel totally confident – I hope. In almost forty years, I am still way short of real competence and confidence. There is an element of bluff and blunder about every decision I make. There is too much to learn. If you ever think you have got it all sorted, give up. You have become a grave danger to yourself.

There is much to be said for running a portfolio on paper for a while before you actually invest any hard cash. Pick a share, learn what you can about it, and follow it for a while. Watch the way the price responds to news, how it moves on bad days and good ones, that sort of thing.

Ultimately, though, in a fast-moving market, there will be a temptation to get in and go. You may not lose anything by standing and watching, but you will never make anything either. So accept what you are doing, why you are looking at punting in the market. You are never going to become an instant expert. Things change so fast that you may never be an expert. Once again, accept that you are gambling. Unless you are very lucky, you will pick some losers. But understand that you are there to learn by experience and are struggling to understand – in stark contrast to some paper pundits who can tell you what to do without ever buying or selling shares themselves.

### *Uncle Warren Buffett and the basics*

Inevitably, when you start making any effort to assess what shares to buy, you will stumble across ideas about "investment fundamentals" and "value investing". This is a fine old-fashioned stew, brought to the boil in recent years by the devotees of Warren Buffett, one of the world's richest men, and arguably the world's most successful investor. He runs a quoted American company called Berkshire Hathaway. Over thirty years or so, he has done brilliantly. Paradoxically, his investment performance has declined in the past five years just as his fame as an investor has reached global proportions.

Most of what he has to say is eminently sensible. A whole industry has been created around his ideas, with books quoting his every utterance, and followers popping up everywhere to tell us how the great man would have seen this and that. Buffett himself admits he was influenced by Benjamin Graham, a fund manager who wrote "The Intelligent Investor", which he calls by far the best book on investing ever written. It was first published in 1949 and draws upon work published in the thirties. It does direct itself at the investor rather than the speculator, and that distinction is highly relevant. The book has no chapter on selling shares, a notion which largely seems to have eluded Graham. Buffett, too, pays relatively little attention to selling, preferring to advocate finding sound companies and sticking with them for the long term.

That is a fatal weakness. The way to make really big money in the stock market may well be to buy sound shares and hold them for several years, while the business builds. You can do that when you have a comfortable capital cushion. That is not what the £1,000 share punter is all about. Medium to long term investment – anything over two years – is a luxury the small money player cannot afford. If you are not making it in the shorter term as a speculator, you are losing ground.

The idea that you should identify a good, long-term growth company and sit with it until it comes right makes pretty remarkable assumptions by most standards. How can you be sure you have picked the right one? How long do you give it ? If it falls by 25pc, how do you know that is not a sign of trouble, and you are not aboard the good long-term growth opportunity you imagined? Those with plenty of cash can risk being wrong. Smaller investors do not have that luxury. They need to keep their capital moving – and cannot afford to see it going nowhere while the market is rising. There is something called opportunity cost – the price you pay for missing opportunities. Think about it.

The idea of "value investing" revolves around selecting companies which are considered sound and solid, with a record of growing profits over the long term, a strong place in the market, and assets which exceed their share values. Nothing wrong with that. If you can find such companies, they should form the backbone of any medium to long term portfolio.

In reality, it is not easy to discover them. The Graham/Buffett criteria are too tough for modern times. Markets these days are too well-researched. Every professional knows what each of the bigger companies owns, where it operates, what profits to expect, and where the opportunities lie, and values the shares accordingly. If you come across a company which looks cheap on such criteria, you will not have made a super discovery. You will have missed something. There will be a snag the market knows about, and that is why the shares seem cheap.

There are few secrets among the top companies. There will sometimes be surprises, things which go wrong, great new deals which can be done, perhaps unexpected bids in the offing. Big companies can make you money sometimes. You might even manage to spot a change in market thinking – share fashion is as fickle as skirt lengths.

Attempts at "value investing" brought some major players real problems in the late nineties as the companies which appeared to qualify under such criteria performed poorly. A rise of 18pc in the Footsie, the index of the top 100 shares, for the whole of 1999 actually concealed a real split – about a third of the companies, mostly those with technology links, did well. The rest lagged. Leaders like Marks & Spencer, GUS, Sainsbury, Railtrack and drinks group Allied Domecq all fared badly. Many of the very best performers met none of the "value investing" criteria. They were internet –related stocks which reported large trading losses and had little in the way of hard assets. But punters loved them and sent prices soaring.

"Value investing" then is not what the small punter wants – but that is not to say that it is safe to ignore the basic rules of investment. Where possible, it is better to buy a share with good profits, plenty of cash, and strong assets.

Best to have a simple working knowledge of the main conventional measures of share value, like –

Profits. There are several forms of profits – operating profits, trading profits, pre-tax profits, net profits, profits after tax, etc

The two most widely used are pre-tax profits – the profit left after deducting everything except tax – and net profits – what is left after deducting everything including tax.

Net profits are usually quickly translated in earnings, or earnings per share. This is a way of dividing the profits after tax into the number of shares, and expressing it as so many pence per share. Put crudely, if you have profits after tax of £100, and there are 100 shares, then there will be earnings of 100p (earnings are normally expressed in pence, not pounds and pence) per share.

Dividends are normally paid out of earnings, and can be expressed as so many pence per share, or as a percentage of the nominal value of the share. Shares can have almost any nominal value. Many have a nominal value of £1, many others 5p, and yet more a nominal value of 1p. It does not really matter. Just because a share has a nominal value of £1, it does not mean it is worth £1. What matters is the price it sells for. So a share with £1 nominal value could sell for 4p, just as one with a nominal value of 5p could sell for £9.

The dividend yield is a way of expressing the annual return you would get in dividends with the shares at a particular price. So if a share at 100p pays a dividend of 10p, the yield (annual return) is 10p divided by 100p, or 10pc. As share prices rise, the yield effectively falls, because you have to pay more to "buy" the same dividend. So at 200p, our 10p a share dividend is worth just 5pc.

Dividends do matter, particularly to long term holders and older investors who rely on income, and they are employed as a measure of value for shares. The most widely used means of a comparison, though, is the price earnings ratio, or pe.

This takes the earnings (net profits earned for each share), and divides them into the share price, thus calculating the number of years it would take for the company to earn the equivalent to the share price in profits. So a share with earnings of 10p, priced at 100p, would sell on a pe of 10. A share with earnings of 10p selling at 200p would have a pe of 20.

Applying these standard measures is common sense. The bigger the profits, and the faster they are growing, the better. High dividend yields are nice, but will normally signal that a share is considered to have poor growth prospects. A low price earnings ratio is attractive, but only if you think the market has it wrong, and the company has prospects which really warrant a higher one. As ever, most shares sell on a low pe for a good reason. So a share with a low dividend yield and a high pe might appear fully-valued, but might be a much better bet than the high-yielder, simply because it has the chance of going somewhere. Sorry to keep slipping in words like "simply". None of it is really that simple – beneath the surface there are all sorts of variations which influence prices.

Then there is the little matter of assets. The assets are the things the company owns. They can be cash, buildings, land, machines, brand names, or even the rights to a good idea. Cash you can understand, though when you try to check that, do not forget to knock off debts. Buildings may be good, but machinery is more doubtful. The company may be valuing it as something near cost, when the second hand value may be nil. Stocks – piles of unsold stuff that the company has made – may be worth a great deal, or practically nothing. Whisky generally gains value as it matures, while no-one wants a store of 1999 diaries.

Cash or near-cash is best. Most companies, in fact, have more borrowings than cash. That is nothing to worry about, so long as the debt is not much greater than the apparent worth of all of the assets – though even that may be irrelevant in technology companies.

What counts most is cash flow and cash burn – the amount of cash coming into the company versus the cash going out. Many companies with books full of orders and products of apparent promise have gone bust because they have run out of cash. They did not have the money to make the goods to meet the orders, and could not borrow enough to keep going until sales were made and the money actually started coming in. In younger companies – the bio-tech and internet operators in particular – it is important to look at the cash in hand, and the borrowing facilities, and measure them against the rate at which the company is spending money – the cash burn. A company with £2m in the bank, a chunk of debt, but no significant orders or assets to borrow against will run out of money in ten months if it is spending £200,000 a month on research and development, unless it can sell something – or persuade a new investor to put more money in. I talk more about this later, but cash is king. Keep an eye out for it in any share you may think of buying.

Profits, yields, price earnings ratios, assets and cash flow are all major elements in knowing how to value shares. The more understanding of them you can develop, the better. But this is not the book to tackle them in detail. They are more important to the longer term player, not the short-term punter. If you want to learn more – you will as you get more into the game – try one of my other books "How To Make A Killing In The Share Jungle", or "How To Make A Killing In Penny Shares". Perhaps the best guide, though, is the Investors Chronicle "Beginners' Guide to Investment" by Bernard Gray. Pretty comprehensive and deeply boring, it is always handy to have around.

# THREE

## GETTING INTO THE ACTION

Hard to believe I just did that – despatched most of the investment fundamentals in a few thousand words, less than a chapter. Tut, tut. It felt good, though, cutting through the undergrowth and getting to the real action more quickly.

In truth, you may not want to spend too much time worrying over profits, accounts, cash flow and so on if you really are one of the £1,000 share punters. Real share gamblers want little more than a name, and the chance to convince themselves that it will bring them a winning bet. And because tens of thousand of City folk are employed to spend their days poring over accounts and analysing the fine detail in the figures, stuff which involves standard investment theory may not be where the real excitement is. Too many shares are too well-known to deliver any great surprises, especially on the up-side. Conventional analysis never expects investors to double their money in a few months.

The real way to a killing in the share jungle is to buy the shares everyone wants before they realise they want them. Successful investment is about anticipation – spotting opportunities before the herd. Then spotting which way the herd will move before it starts to shift.

### *Weight of money*

Take a step back. The weight of money is what really determines the direction of share prices. More in than out, and up the price goes. Get in early and other investors will push the price up for you as they join in. In this example, of course, "early" is a relative term. You will never get there first, never spot the chance before absolutely everyone else. If you do, it might not help. No good being the only one in the crowd to spot a massive bargain, the one soldier marching in step. If no-one else spots your winner, you will be left sitting on your own, wondering why nothing is happening, forever. Unless others get the message and start to buy, your undervalued bargain will stay undervalued, and your bargain might be a loser after all.

At this point, I trust, a light popped on for anyone who uses the internet. Suddenly there is a brilliant means of communication available to everyone on the net. Pop your thoughts on some internet investment bulletin board, and traders all over the world can see them. There may be folk up there ramping shares quite deliberately, but way the net can be used to exchange ideas opens a whole new dimension to investors – and the small investor is up there leading the way. Terrific.

### *Momentum*

Never worry about leaping aboard a bandwagon once it has started rolling. Momentum is a wondrous thing in the share game. Once prices start to rise, people begin to notice, check what the action is all about, and then join the fun. It is surprising how far that can take a share before something happens to halt the rise and slam it into reverse.

You do not have to be a great original to make money in shares. I doubt if I have ever had a truly original thought in my investment life. I read, and talk, and watch, pinch other people's ideas, and run with the ones which make sense to me. The trick is to get aboard early enough in the game, when there is plenty of room for others to follow. And – crucially – to get out early enough so that there are still buyers ready to take your shares and allow you to sell at a profit.

### *Action*

Action is essential. You want a company where things are happening, where there is a solid news-flow. No good sitting there with nothing happening for most of the year. You want something to look forward to – something to keep everyone interested. Some of it comes with the routine company calendar.

### *Preliminary statement*

The conventional company year is well-defined. You get a preliminary statement of the profits for the year (otherwise know as "the results"). Obviously that comes once every 12 months. In a decent company, it should come within two months of the year-end.

### *Report and accounts*

A few weeks later, the company should send out the annual report and accounts. That is normally prepared well in advance, and though it is meat and drink to the analyst community and those who pore over the detail, for the short term player, it might not have that much excitement. Look at it carefully, though, for all of those conventional investment yard-sticks – the level of debt, how much cash there is in the company, how exceptional and extraordinary items distorted profits, and so on. Do read the fine print, including the accounting notes. You will gradually get the hang of them.

### *Auditors report*

Most important, check whether there is any qualification to the auditors report. That should say the accounts conform to the Companies Act and so on. Any significant qualification to that is a real warning – stay clear.

### *Directors' share stakes*

Take a look at the directors' share stakes, and check whether they have changed. Look to see whether they have been buyers or sellers, or have been granted extra options to buy shares. All the way, you are looking for clues as to what price they traded at, or at which they get extra shares. It will give a clue to their expectations.

### *Outside shareholders*

Look, too, to see whether the list of main outside shareholders has changed. Anyone above 3pc or so ought to be declared. You want to know who these people are, whether they are associated with the board, and thus help control the company (over 50pc of the shares is obvious control, over 29.9pc is deemed control by the Takeover Panel. Anything approaching 20pc should stand as pretty nearly enough control so far as you are concerned)

Read everything. What you are trying to do is to gain a greater understanding of what the company actually does. More important, you are looking for clues about new developments, something which will impact upon the share price if it goes well or badly.

### *Notice of annual meeting*

Oh, and though it is a bore, study the notice of the annual meeting carefully. Try to trace any references it may make to this article of association or that. Mostly it will be insignificant. But these dry lines can sometimes contain quite important clues. They might conceal a change in share option prices.

### *Pre-emption rights*

Quite often, there will be a disapplication of pre-emption rights. This may sound obscure, but could be worth watching. Mostly it will allow the board to issue extra shares without first consulting shareholders. If that deals with small amounts – say up to 15pc – that is routine. It might involve many more shares. The internet incubator companies in particular have been seeking the right to issue loads of shares, hundreds of millions sometimes, when they like. On the whole, this is good. In theory, it means shareholders surrender some notional control over what is going on. In practice, it probably means the directors are planning a big acquisition and want to use shares. Or they are planning another big fund-raising at some stage. Either way, when the market is running, it should be good. It means there is action in the offing – just what you want.

### *Annual meeting*

There must be at least 21 days notice of the annual meeting in the report and accounts. If you can, go along. Do not be late. Most of these meetings are over inside ten minutes. The better ones, though, are seen by the directors as an opportunity to meet and impress shareholders. So you should get the chance to talk to directors face to face. You can size them up – the best way of establishing whether your investment makes sense – and you might get a much better feel for what they are trying to do. Sometimes directors reveal the most extraordinary plans when they are actually chatting to people. Remember, though, that this is the ideal chance for them to shower you with over-optimistic rubbish, and to try to con you. So be careful. Every con-artist will have a plausible story. Otherwise he never gets to first base.

### *Interim results*

Maybe three or four months after the annual meeting, most companies announce their interim results. These cover progress at the half-year. They obviously form an important news event, and could impact upon the share price. You need to watch out for them. Try to establish – from the company secretary, or the company brokers – roughly when the interim or any announcement is due. The boys in the market will be watching and waiting for them. Shares frequently move in advance of any announcement, and unless the news is better than expected (whether it be good or bad news), the price might slip a little.

### *Insider trading*

Nine times out of ten may be overstating the incidence of insider trading, but three or four out of five would not. In the majority of cases, the market or a part of it knows pretty well what is going to be in any announcement. Someone talks, and someone deals. No point in getting into the morality or legality of it here. Obviously it is immoral, and mostly it is illegal. Too bad. If the idea upsets you, do not trade in shares.

Accept it, and try to use it. Remember the rule about listening to what the market tells you? Someone always knows, and often someone deals. So watch which way the shares are moving ahead of any announcement. That will give you a clue as to whether the news is good or bad. If it is moving up, sometimes it will be best to sell in advance, because the good news will be in the price. That is not a firm rule, however. Really good news, once it reaches everyone, could take the price much higher.

Bad news might be a little different. If the shares start easing ahead of an announcement, it might make sense to sell. The company will have made a greater effort to keep bad news secret, so those who do know and are acting will be in a tighter circle, and will be taking more risk when they sell. So perhaps bad news will have more impact when it is actually announced. In any case, if you are a short term punter, you do not want to be in a share which is easing. You certainly do not want to be in one which might be signalling problems which could prompt a sharper fall in the price.

Back we go to the basic rule – if in doubt, sell out. You are not around for the longer ride, the fall and then the slow recovery. Knock it out, take your cash, and play somewhere else. There is no such thing as loyalty to a company, or a share. All you want is a profit, not a knighthood for services to some ailing industry.

These rules about insider trading and how to use them apply to any sort of share action, conventional profits announcements, bid rumours, anything. Obviously in the case of bid rumours, the moves can be more volatile, and the mood can change from day to day. Companies do change their mind in the middle of bids, and sometimes those who think they are dealing with privileged information find they have been sold a wrong steer, and come a cropper. So movements in advance of bid stories are less reliable indicators. Watch them, all the same.

### *More Action*

Aside from the standard company announcements calendar, you could see news of bids and deals, board appointments, new orders, share stakes, and so on. They all supply evidence that the company is alive, and aware of a duty to shareholders to keep them in touch. The nature of those announcements is self-evident, and need no great discussion here. Obviously anything is worth looking at carefully – the background of a new director, the potential in any deal, the strength of any bid approach, the names behind any new holder of a share stake. Watch the financial press for comments, and scan the internet bulletin boards.

There is a pretty fine line between too much action, and just enough. It is hard to know where to draw it. Perhaps the best clue is in the nature of those announcements. It is tempting to say the more, the merrier, but that is not always right. You want your board to be alive to shareholder interest, but not to spend their time pumping out bullish statements which end up looking like an attempt to pump the share price. If they have a decent stake in the company – and they should – they will be every bit as interested as you in getting the price up. Now and then, though, that is almost all they are interested in.

Some boys do get into the business with the aim of making a quick share price killing, and then bowing out with the cash. Usually they have to sell the whole company to do it, and that will suit the outside investors as well. Now and then, though, they do manage to filter out stock in quite large quantities before they have negotiated anything of consequence for the company. Or they might be simply trying to pump the share price up so that they can do some deal. That does not always work. They will be playing against other company directors who understand the game pretty well, and if the pumping operation should fail, the shares will slump.

### *Public Relations*

This section is particular fun, because readers should know that I left the Daily Mail in October 1998 to become a director of a financial public relations company called Square Mile Communications. One of the main reasons I went there was because it seemed to be staffed by sensible people doing sensible things, not trying too hard to influence journalists and pump attention up in the wrong way. That view of Square Mile has not changed, and I only mention the connection here because you ought to know about it in this context.

Good financial public relations is essential to any listed company with a trace of ambition. Companies have a duty to keep investors properly informed, and those that neglect it tend to see their share prices slip quietly back as the business fades from view. Though the market in small company shares perked up wonderfully in 1999, it is difficult to generate proper attention for small companies. Newspapers, reasonably enough, concentrate on the bigger boys because they know more readers are likely to be interested in them. It follows that the bigger companies have more shareholders, more employees, and more chance of doing bigger money deals.

The pressure on newspaper space is enormous, and proper public relations involves trying to ensure that all media are made aware and kept aware of what is going on in client companies. It does not involve pushing journalists to write favourable pieces all of the time – though there is a degree of that, and inevitably, there is some attempt to distract attention from bad news, or to play it down.

Any investor wants to see a good financial public relations operation in the background for any company. At the most basic, this should ensure that any news is made available to all forms of media, and is presented intelligibly. Good financial public relations will also try to ensure that appropriate journalists know the company directors, and that any comment is written with the benefit of an informed view, preferably from the company.

### *Web sites*

In the last resort, investors should contact the public relations company for information. Ideally, most companies should have their own web site. That should carry full details of any announcements, and the pr company ought to be able to direct investors to it, or perhaps display the announcements on the pr company web site. You might find the address of the web site in the annual accounts. Most companies will send you a copy of the accounts. Ask the company secretary at the registered office.

### *Company brokers*

Every public company has to have a firm of stockbrokers advising it. They are known as the house brokers, or the shop. They will usually have an analyst following the company, and producing research notes and profit forecasts on the company. You want to see those notes, that information, getting around the market and generating action. Naturally, anything from the company broker is expected to err somewhat on the supportive side, though is generally expected to be pretty accurate. In a way, because they are restricted by closer contact with the company, house brokers may tend to be a touch more conservative in their forecasts than some outsiders. The company will normally want to keep published predictions in check, because they know it makes more sense to surprise on the upside than to disappoint.

As an outsider, unless you happen to be looking at a stock covered by your own broker, you might find it hard to gain access to those forecasts. By all means ring and ask for a copy of any written work. You might get lucky. Happily, there are now a number of publications which cover most broking forecasts. The Hemmington Scott site has access to Company Refs, which carries brief details of most forecasts. There is also the Estimate Directory. Poke about. You will probably find most of these on-line.

They will give you a fair idea of what is going on, but probably not the full story. Most brokers will not give you access to their internal notes, the kind of stuff which analysts read to salesmen at morning meetings, and which is then circulated inside the firm. This is closer to the real thing. It will carry information about any changes in profit forecasts first, and break the news about fresh trading developments. That, in turn, will be fed by the sales force to the big customers, the institutional traders.

### *Privileged information*

It is a form of privileged information, probably inside information if you were to apply a strict rule. But almost everyone does it. Companies do not like to surprise the market. They generally try to give them an idea in advance of the way things are going. They manage the news flow, especially if it is negative. All brokers – the shop or outsiders – are in the habit of submitting drafts of circulars on the company to the company secretary, finance director, or even chief executive for comment. Companies respond to varying degrees. Legend has it that some virtually re-write passages they are unhappy with, or put in appropriate figures. Others give a nudge here and there.

Small investors are dealing very much behind the real action, then, in many companies. Do not worry. This happens most actively in the big ones, the ones which will generally be of less concern to the small share punter. The system is much less active among smaller companies. They are sometimes lucky to keep the mandatory one broker on side. Often those brokers will not have got around to writing a circular. Some will have only a token analyst or two, feeding information to the biggest clients, and may not even give any serious coverage to some of the smaller companies. That helps make them a more fertile field for the private investor.

### *Brokers' circulars*

Despite this, brokers' circulars are part of the action you want to see. You want to know someone is out there, helping spread understanding about the company. The more the merrier. If you live outside London, and know a local company has links to a local broking office, pester them. They should have some sort of circular, or might direct you to one.

### *Stock market reports*

One of the best places for picking up this sort of action is in the market reports which most newspapers carry each day. To my mind, the market reporter is almost the most important writer on the page. It is not a criticism to say that market reporters are not paid to analyse stocks, to spot the winners and the duds. That is not their job. They are employed to pick up what is happening in the market, and report it to readers.

A good market reporter – and out of the 1999 batch that includes Geoff Foster on the Mail, Francesco Guerrera (or the veteran Derek Pain) on the Independent, and Mickey Clarke of the London Evening Standard – will gather the bid rumours, pick up on the latest circulars, or snatches of what the salesmen in broking houses are telling clients, and keep track of what share stakes are on the move. They are fed information by all sorts of characters around the market, and by public relations people anxious to get across a story which they cannot officially announce. As a long term Daily Man man, I should in fairness say that The Daily Express City section under Robert Miller is worth watching, and employs some expert, experienced market reporters.

Do not expect detailed analysis in market reports. Some of the stories are improbable. No-one tells a financial journalist anything without an ulterior motive. The teller wants the story to get out, for one reason or another. Sometimes the market boys are completely legged over, and fall for stories which are deliberately fed to them to suit someone's dealing position. It would be naïve to expect anything else. But a good market reporter is worth his weight in Scotch. They get wind of a high proportion of bids and deals, and can give valuable clues as to what is really going on.

### *A note of caution*

Happily, the red top tabloids are catching up with the City and beginning to understand that the fun and games in share prices is growing more appealing to their readers. They are at last beginning to recruit relatively well-informed financial journalists who know a thing or two, and not simply dumping the job on anyone who will take it. That is excellent, and to be applauded. In 1999, though, one or two of them got carried away by their own exuberance. The City Slickers in the Mirror, in particular, printed some good tips, but also ran a few stories which were wildly out of whack. So be careful. The City sniffs at the City coverage in The Mirror and The Sun. That is a mistake. It is beginning to get there, and could become a force to be reckoned with. The big circulation tabloids are beginning to appreciate that their readers like playing the market, and want ideas. No wonder the City pages are generally close to the racing pages.

# FOUR

# *THE BOYS AND THEIR TOYS*

Never mind the nonsense about corporate governance, committees on every company to watch executive pay, to balance executive directors with non-executives, count the ash-trays, and such. People are what make a successful company, and the most successful of all are often driven by one or two dominant personalities. According to some Stock Exchange and Government-endorsed directives, the office of chairman and chief executive should be split. No-one should be allowed to fill both posts. Instead we should have a proper balance, one restraining and advising the other.

All very nice in theory, and jolly suitable for those big, boring businesses most small share punters will want to avoid. The Cadbury, Greenbury and Hampel reports gave gangs of highly paid people something to keep them busy, and took them away from running their companies for a while. And the stuff about having an adequate number of non-executive directors made it fine to pass around a few plum jobs to your pals, in the sure knowledge that the knowing nod you give comes back to you as a handy £20,000 a year sinecure when you retire from the big one. As a small shareholder, who needs it?

The small company punter depends crucially on the players, the boys who get into smaller companies, load up with shares, options, warrants and other toys and devote themselves to making money for themselves by shunting the shares higher. Simple.

## *Greed is good*

What you want is a greedy, determined man – or team – committed to making things happen. No moral judgements apply. Just make sure that whatever the boys are doing to make money for themselves is channelled into the share price. Greed is good for the £1,000 share punter. Ride along with it, enjoy it.

It takes an enormous amount of energy and commitment to build a successful company. There was a while when it appeared sensible not to buy shares in a business where the boss was under thirty or over sixty. That has changed. Avoiding companies run by the over-sixties still holds good, but in the internet era, it is hard to know where to draw the line at the bottom. Several men – and a few women – are emerging as significant movers at the head of internet companies when they are barely into their twenties.

They have the energy, vision and total commitment needed to make such businesses work. In these early internet days, it is hard to form any real judgement of them. You can read the interviews, but they rarely give too strong a glimpse of how these people will fare over the longer term – say three or four years out. You simply have to take them on trust. The one real example of a young media star who has put a few years in at the end of 1999 is Dan Wagner, the man behind information group Dialog, or Dial-A-Dog as it has become known around the market. The nick-name says it all. Slick young Dan flashed and sparkled, overflowing with ideas. He has built the company, kept it rolling for a few years, and changed the nature of it significantly. But he has burdened the business with massive debt which has crippled the share price through the late nineties. Whatever else he has done, Dan has not emerged as the shareholders' friend.

## *The record*

The new breed of internet millionaires are hard to judge as individuals. The best you can hope to do is to get their measure by looking at the other players around them, the rest of the team. It is sad to say it, but the presence of a grey hair or two might be some comfort – though I know of at least one where the board of twenty and thirty somethings is clearly at odds with the fifty something they have grafted on to give them more City appeal. They try to say the right words, but clearly betray a massive generation gap.

Elsewhere, there is no substitute for looking at the record of the players. In the most absurd demonstration of how a powerful reputation can pay off, tiny shell company Knutsford went soaring when four well-known players climbed aboard in the summer of 1999. Archie Norman built his name as a director of Woolworth owner Kingfisher, then moved in to turn supermarket group Asda around. Nigel Wray moved from running a tip sheet into what became Carlton Communications, and became the brain behind a large number of small companies as he bought in and developed them by a series of deals. Nick Leslau was the property ace who join Wray along the way, and helped create several highly successful businesses. And Julian Richer built the Richer Sound audio equipment retailing company, developing a reputation as a highly successful staff motivator.

When these four moved into Knutsford, a shell with assets of £5m, they sent the shares soaring one hundred-fold. Take into account the warrants the boys could exercise eventually to give themselves more shares, and the whole shebang was valued at around £1.5bn without doing a thing. As 2000 dawns, there are rumours that Knutsford will bid for any number of troubled shop chains from Storehouse to Marks & Spencer. None of it makes real sense in shareholder value terms. But as a tribute to the reputation of the famous four, it is massive. More important, it demonstrates that having the right names aboard, even if they do little, can be enormously valuable.

Records matter. So when it comes to selecting a company to buy, check what the boys on the board have been doing. If there has been a share offering of any sort – either a flotation prospectus or a significant rights issue – there will be a document carrying details of what the directors did before. It should also have a list of past directorships. Read them carefully. Obviously you want to know that your board is packed with players who have made money before. Failing that, you want to see directors who have had experience with successful companies, perhaps below board level, and are now striking out, trying to make money by running their own show.

### *The advisers*

When you do this, look at the advisers, too. There will be investment banks and brokers in the background. The bigger they are, the better. Try to check what successful companies these people have been associated with, and watch out for duds. If they have had more than one failure, seriously consider staying clear. It is remarkable how success breeds success, and vice versa. Well, perhaps not so remarkable. The best businesses will naturally have the best advisers knocking on their door, wanting to help them make money. The weaker the business, the more likely it is to have to settle for second-rate backers.

It is not hard to find out who the backers may be. They show up in documents, and in all sorts of reference books, from Company Refs to those quarterly company registers you can find in many libraries, or even in The AIM Guide published by the Growth Company Investor. Once you have identified the advisers, it is not quite so easy to find out what else they have been involved in. Try something called Crawfords Directory of City Connections.

Perhaps the Corporate Register sponsored by the insanely named PriceWaterhouseCoopers is most useful of all. It has a brief section on most quoted companies, and another useful chunk giving a potted history of many directors. And it lists financial advisers and their clients. Very handy. Published quarterly, you will not want to buy it. But your broker might have a copy. Or your public library.

### *Shareholdings*

Once you know who you might be dealing with, get down to seeing how greedy they might be. If they are to make serious money for you, it is important to make sure they are committed to making serious money for themselves. No good if the boys at the top are just incredibly superior wage slaves, pulling £1m or so a year out of the company, and sitting with £100,000 or so of shares.

What is their real motivation? Making a fortune for the company and the shareholders? Or lining their own pockets without taking too much risk? Perhaps the grand committees, the Cadbury, the Greenbury and the Hampel, have got it wrong. They are encouraging the growth of businesses which are themselves run by committees of chaps who can do very nicely, thank you, by keeping the engine ticking over. So long as they do not get anything too wrong, they sit in chauffeur-driven luxury, insulated by £1m plus salaries from the real world. So long as they do not break the law, they know they will be let down gently if they get it wrong.

There will be golden parachutes, fat-cat compensation schemes, exceptional payments into their pensions, if they should be asked to leave. They have no great amount, in proportion to their pay packets, riding on the share price. If that collapses, it hurts the shareholders more than the directors.

That hardly sounds like a formula for building a dramatically good business. It might help keep companies ticking over reasonably nicely, but not much more in many cases.

Far better for the short term punter to get behind some chancer whose life depends on shifting the share price skywards. It is not just cash – though that is vitally important – in many cases it is ambition, ego, and a whole lot else rolled into one. Hunger for success, greed if you like, is what often helps build a better business. Or creates a faster-rising share price.

So scan the share list. What you want is a board loaded with shares from the start, taking more shares on every deal they can, and weighing in with extra options every year. What do you care if they end up making tens of millions, so long as you double or treble your money ? Or more ?

Check the list quite carefully. Sometimes you might get a surprise. The man up front, doing all the talking, might not be the boy with the most shares. The one with the stock is the one to watch.

## *Share options*

Option schemes are important. They are everywhere in small, growing companies these days. The more options, the greedier the board, the better. Up to a point. They should be able to earn more linked to share price targets. They should be relatively demanding targets. Here we are not talking about the soaraway stock markets of the last quarter of 1999, when some prices rocketed eight to ten fold in a few weeks. In more normal conditions, it is reasonable to see extra options weighing in when the price has doubled in, say, a year or two. If the boys do that, any way, they will have deserved extra.

It is even a good sign when the board asks for extra options. So long as they are only exercisable - the boys get the shares – if they have pushed the price ahead far enough, applaud it. It is a sign of ambition. It means that they think they can get the shares up, and by golly, if they do, they want rewarding for it. Terrific. Far better that than some sleepy old team content to take a fat pay cheque each month and forget the shares. You do well for me, I do well by you. It works for everyone.

### *Exploding options*

It is possible to overdo this – just. Damian Aspinall, Dan Taylor and some of the boys behind Cambury Investments – now e-Capital – did just that. They got too greedy. They created a nice shell, a quoted company with nothing but cash in it, ready to buy a business. But they constructed such rich options for themselves that no-one would deal. It would have meant that any successful business going into Cambury would have surrendered too many shares to Aspinall et al as the price grew. Only when they modified the so-called exploding options did they get someone to agree to start deals. Then the name changed to e-Capital, we had a new internet incubator fund, and the game was on.

### *Warrants*

Even then, e-Capital was burdened with rather too many warrants for complete comfort. Warrants are little bits of paper, usually traded separately from the Ordinary shares. These carry the right to subscribe for new shares in the company at a set price on set dates in the future. For the company, they mean that a rise in the share price can encourage people to exercise the warrants, effectively putting extra capital into the company in exchange for new shares. The issue of extra shares at what are usually low rates does serve to dilute the interests of existing shareholders, so the scheme has disadvantages. Anyone buying the warrants can do rather well, however. Because the warrants will trade for less than the Ordinary shares, buyers can effectively gamble on the shares rising without paying the full price for those shares. More bang for less buck – a process known as gearing.

The main snag for such gamblers is that if the share price does not rise far enough to make the warrants worth exercising in the allotted time, then warrants can become worthless. Say, for example, you have a warrant to buy shares in Bloggs at 5p in June 2001 or June 2002. If Bloggs shares rise to 10p before June 2001, the warrants should be worth perhaps 5 1/2p – made up of the 5p gain over the 5p price at which new shares can be bought, plus 1/2p for the time they allow you to gamble on a still greater gain. But if Bloggs shares are only 4p come June 2002, the warrants will be worthless. No-one will want the right to buy new Bloggs shares for 5p when they can buy them in the market for 4p.

Trading warrants can also be riskier because there are usually far fewer of them than there are Ordinary shares. That means the market in them will be tighter – it is harder to buy or sell at sensible prices in reasonable quantities. So you could get stuck with virtually unsaleable warrants, if you are unlucky.

### *Dilution*

On a more general note, if a company has too many warrants in relation to the issued Ordinary capital, it can be bad news. If you know, for example, that there are warrants enough to double the issued capital in six months, you will worry about dilution, the impact that the new capital issue will have on the share price. The market could be almost swamped with new shares, and the price could be driven lower. Not to mention that doubling the capital at a lower price will dilute the asset value of the existing shares. Say the market value of the issued capital was £1m in 100p nominal Ordinary shares, and the assets were £1m. Each, say, Ordinary share selling at 100p would be backed by assets of 100p. Assume that the issued capital was doubled as warrant holders exercised their rights to buy new shares at 50p. Suddenly the issued capital would be £2m, but the asset value would have gone up by only £500,000 to £1.5m. Each share would be backed by assets of only 75p. The former warrant holders would have done well, but the Ordinary shareholders would have seen their asset backing reduced – diluted. The share price would fall, probably to around 75p.

### *Count the capital*

This simple example can be important, even to the short term punter. When prices are moving far and fast, it is tough to keep track of things. But the dilution factor was in play late in 1999 among some of the internet incubator stocks. Though anyone looking at their total market capitalisation might have assumed they were all valued at about the same level, some were effectively more highly rated than others because there were extra warrants and options hovering in the background. They might not have been exercised, but they could be at some stage, potentially diluting the value of assets for the existing ordinary shareholders. So if you can, count all of the capital. Ask your broker, if you have one you can talk to, about options and warrants. Or check with the secretary of the company itself.

# FIVE

## *NEW ISSUES*

No doubt about it, the hot way to make money fast around the Millennium has been to get into a new issue, preferably at the very beginning.

The profits for punters quick enough or lucky enough to get aboard the right rockets have been quite fantastic. Even forgetting Knutsford – the Norman, Wray, Leslau, Richer vehicle which flashed from 2 1/2p to 250p in a couple of days – there have been some real sensations, especially if they were internet-powered. Just before Christmas, a couple of internet new issues headed by the sons of market veterans traced a dazzling path across the sky. Jim Slater's son Mark heads Internet Indirect. Issued at 5p, the shares touched 90p inside a week, and saw the New Year in at 85p. That made 30 year-old Mark worth £17m on paper, without counting warrants which might treble his share stake if all goes well. JellyWorks, with 24 year-old Jonathan Rowland as chief executive, went from 5p to 112 1/2p in a few days. At that, it was valued at £245m, though it had assets of £9m. Rowland is the son of David Rowland, a controversial property developer who attracted stock market attention himself in the seventies.

Neither Internet Indirect nor JellyWorks had actually done anything before it came to market. They were effectively virgin players, intent on getting into the action. Both unveiled plans to buy into the internet excitement. Hopes and dreams came at a massive premium.

The share gains, though, were real enough. And many small investors piled in, bought the shares on the way up, and quickly doubled their money, or thereabouts, in both within a matter of days. When a sector is hot, it is hot. No point in standing and waiting, bewailing the lack of "fundamental values", and wondering why such youngsters should command a massive premium over a tiny asset value. Both shares clearly felt right to the market at the time.

The problem with such new issues – quite apart from the difficulty in arriving at any rational basis for valuation (more of that elsewhere) – is getting hold of the shares at the start. And that is a real problem.

### *Who gets new issues*

The reality is that most new issues these days go to the folks in the know. That emphatically does not mean most of the small share punters. Indeed, there is a rough and ready rule developing – if you can get the stock, you don't want it.

Gone are the days of Sid and the selling of British Gas shares to anyone who wanted them. The privatisation issues are gone. Nowadays the real goodies are spread around among the boys in the City.

## *Offer for sale*

It used to be that companies floated through an offer for sale. The share issue was widely advertised, and anyone could obtain a prospectus giving details of the company and a form to apply for the shares. Mini-prospectuses were made available, and you could even fill in a coupon in the national newspapers and post it off with a cheque. You might not get all of the shares you wanted, but you could usually count on getting some. They would start life at a handsome premium over the issue price, just as the issuing house intended, and everyone was happy.

Then the boys in the City got more greedy. Apart from the really big money issues, where they would need all they could get, they realised that they were onto a good thing. Far better to spread the gains around among City institutions, the big investors who would scratch their back when the time came. The Stock Exchange, ever alert to the needs of its masters, connived to changes in the rules which gradually meant that fewer and fewer shares in new issues had to be made available to ordinary members of the public. That meant more for the boys. These days, if you see an offer for sale, it probably means the boys in the City do not fancy it much. They will take some, but shunt out as many as they decently can to small investors. Maybe Thomson Holidays had good reason to pull in as many prospective customers as possible by offering them shares in the float. But that was the last major offer for sale in the nineties. And what a flop that has proved. I am ashamed to say that I misjudged it, and urged people to buy. Sorry about that.

There are some new issues available as an Offer for Sale on Ofex, the trading facility run by J.P.Jenkins outside the Stock Exchange rules. There are good opportunities there, but they are more speculative, and must be viewed with great care. More about Ofex elsewhere.

### *Placings*

Nowadays, many of the really juicy issues take the form of placings. The issuing house effectively agrees to find buyers for the shares on behalf of the company. So the shares all go to those on a list of investors known to the company or the brokers concerned. Chase your broker and ask him to see if he can get your name on the list, and you might get a few if you are lucky – very lucky. Only if you happen to deal through the broking house sponsoring the issue will you stand any real chance of getting aboard – and then you will probably get scaled back massively on any decent issue.

### *Intermediaries offers*

You should stand a rather better chance with what is called an intermediaries offer. This is more or less the same as a placing, but the chances of getting a few if you ask your broker to apply are somewhat greater. The best chance is if you can get on the list of an intermediary which does a regular flow of such offers. If you can get in on one, you tend to get the offer of others.

### *Information sources*

Whatever the new issue, you can only improve your chances by acting early. So you need to watch out for details of potential flotations. Keep an eye on the City pages for random comments, and ask your broker to keep you in touch (some make a point of offering new issue help). People like Hargreaves Lansdown have tried to make special efforts to get investors into new issues.

The Financial Mail on Sunday runs a regular chart detailing forthcoming flotations, and usually carries the name and phone number of the sponsor. The Investors Chronicle has a longer list, but it is often short on detail.

### *Evaluating new issues*

Though most new issues in the second half of 1999 have gone well, regardless of the quality of the underlying business, it would be stupid to suggest you should buy anything you can get. Sooner or later, the fashion for internet stocks will pass, and the buying frenzy will fade. If circumstances seem right, and you are looking to "stag" an issue – buy at the issue price and sell at a premium on the first day or two of dealing – then quality issues are not quite so important. Even then, though, they do matter. You do not want to be left with a load of shares in an issue which has struggled to attract subscribers, and which will open at a discount. That does happen. It has happened quite frequently when the market has been out of sorts. So instead of a quick profit, you end up with an embarrassing loss, or a bundle of shares you really do not want to hold, just hanging on, waiting in the hope that they will rise and let you out with your money back.

In order to decide which to go for, which to leave, much of it comes down to the players – the directors and their history, and the strength of the financial advisers – and how deeply they are committed personally through the number of shares they have themselves, or their options package.

### *The free float*

One of the most crucial elements in determining whether a new issue will fly or flop is probably among the most overlooked – the free float. This is simply the number of shares which are being made available to the market. Rarely does it attract comment from those who write about new issue prospects, but several shrewd players and their advisers have cottoned onto this one and used it to the maximum advantage in 1999.

Stands to reason that the fewer shares on sale, the higher buyers will push the price to get hold of them.We are assuming, of course, that the issue is half-decent to begin with – or at least, that sufficient people can be persuaded to believe it is one they should buy. The most perfect example to come to the Alternative Investment Market was a company called Jetcam International. This makes software for metal forming machinery, and looks a genuinely attractive business. Only around 2pc of the capital was made available to the market in the issue. No wonder it opened at a handsome premium.

If you checked some of the new internet stars, you would have found that relatively few shares were on offer. Large chunks were held by offshore trusts. It did not take much buying by eager investors to ensure that the opening price went soaring – and stayed up.

What is not generally understood is that certain players have a fan club of investors who will buy whatever they have to sell. And they will be so grateful for getting stock at the low original placing price that they will be sure to go into the market and buy more when trading starts. That ensures that they push the price up further, helping themselves, helping the directors and other existing shareholders who did not sell in the issue, and creating a still greater impression that this is a whiz-bang soaraway company which everyone should pile into. Nothing formal, of course. Just an understanding of how things work.

Anything helps. There will have been a few wry smiles around the market on New Year's Eve when it was revealed that Ed Guinan, the chairman of newest internet incubator star JellyWorks, had bought shares for his children's trusts at between 124p and 137p, peak prices for a company which had floated at 5p a week or so earlier. In the opening days, he bought more than 300,000 shares, on paper delivering a massive boost to the value of his options, if the price can be sustained. Such strong buying helped everyone, since he took some from the trusts of the controlling Rowland family. They had 80pc of the shares, ensuring that the market responded well to relatively modest buying. Guinan's purchases from the trusts ensured that there was no need to sell on the open market, thereby avoiding the risk of pushing the price lower. Oh what fun.

### *Lock-ins*

It would be wrong to suggest, however, that this early action brought immediate riches to the insider shareholders. Happily, the lock-in rules of the Alternative Investment Market mean that they are unable to sell within a year of flotation, except in certain restricted circumstances. That is a real bonus for the outside investors. It ensures that directors and their associates cannot pump the price up and then dump the shares quickly. They have to work to try to ensure that it stays high for at least a year if they are to benefit directly themselves. In some cases, the directors and their advisers accept still tougher terms. In the case of the other pre-Christmas internet flyer, Internet Indirect, the Slater family and the other directors agreed not to dispose of any interests in the securities of the company within the first two years. Excellent.

### *The business plan*

Obviously you also need pay attention to the business plan. Read the prospectus and try to decide whether it makes sense, whether the area the company plans to operate in looks good to you or not. The best way of establishing that is to look at comparative companies, other businesses in the same sort of area. See how they have been doing, and how their shares have performed. If the new issue looks as plausible, perhaps even better, go for it if the shares are priced on a low projected price earnings ratio, and possibly a higher dividend yield. Look, too, at the historic record, if the company has been established for a while. The smoother the growth record, the better in general.

### *Where the money is going*

Most important, check to see where the new money raised in the flotation is going. Especially in cases where the company was bought out of a bigger company by the management a few years ago (a management buy-out or mbo), and has been backed by banks or venture capitalists. Frequently the money being raised in the float will go to paying off the debt the boys took on when they bought the company. Removing that debt will slash interest payments, and could generate a significant, effortless boost in profits and earnings per share. The ability to pump extra money into the operation, either with cash from the float or by opening the way to new borrowings, could also help transform prospects.

### *Read the papers*

Probably the best way of sizing up a new issue, though, is to read the financial press and to talk to your broker. These days, because new issues are generally done by a placing, the newspapers tend not to make such a serious job of assessing the merits of issues. Often they settle for a quick look at the press release, scanning it to see if anyone stands to make a quick fortune, and will not even be sent the full flotation document. Sometimes, though, they do comment on the merits of the float. That comment will be coloured by talking to the advisers to the flotation and perhaps to the company. It may not always be a good guide, but will help. Magazines like the Investors Chronicle also tend to weigh the merits of new issues. Increasingly, there is also comment on the internet bulletin boards, though this needs to be treated with great care, since there is no way of knowing whether the people who post their opinions have any real idea of what they are talking about. The sheer volume of comments on particular issues, though, can give you some idea of their popularity.

Do not ignore comments in newspapers and magazines, and do ask your broker what he is hearing around the City. There is absolutely no point in being the only one in the world who recognises the merits of a particular issue. If you are the only one who applies for the shares, and the rest of the world ignores them, then the issue will flop. There are no marks for being the only one in step. What determines the success of a flotation is the weight of money coming in for it. If the sponsors struggle to attract buyers, the price will not perform, and you do not want to know. If you really are convinced the company is right, wait until dealings start. If the issue is a flop, the price will fall, and you will be able to buy more cheaply in the market.

### *Selling new issues*

If you do manage to get stock in a new issue, and it races away at the opening, think carefully before you sell and take your profit. Much will depend upon the general market mood. In most cases towards the end of 1999, it was wrong to sell quickly. Success can be self-feeding. Shares in a placing start at a big premium, the press notices, and writes about the company. That attracts more attention, and encourages more buyers to come in. So it could well take three or four days before the initial momentum fades. That could be the time to sell.

What is pretty near certain is that the profit in the first three or four days will be proportionately greater than over the following month or so. There are no hard and fast rules in this, but the initial euphoria does fade fairly quickly, and the performance becomes more subdued.

This is not to suggest that the shares will automatically decline. It is more of an arithmetical thing. Assume you have shares in a stock which was placed at 5p, and opens at 30p. You have made six times your money. If you invested £1,000, you will have £6,000. Instead of counting your chickens, rebase your arithmetic. Remind yourself that you now have £6,000 invested in shares at 30p. If they were to match their opening performance, and multiply six-fold, they would rocket to 180p, and your cash commitment would be £36,000. At the end of 1999, there were a few stocks generating such remarkable gains. In truth, though, they were truly exceptional. Anyone would be delighted if that opening six-fold gain became ten-fold. At that stage, your shares would have risen to 50p, and would be worth £50,000 – a handsome performance.

Take a really tough stand, however, and you see that the advance from 30p to 50p is a rise of 66pc, or two-thirds. If you are a real high-flyer, and stocks are racing away all around you, perhaps you should have cashed in on a six-fold rise, and tried to put your cash into another new issue. If you took the £36,000 and doubled it, you would have £72,000, a far better showing than hanging on and making a ten-fold gain from your original starting point.

A silly example? A greedy, unrealistic one? Perhaps. Accept that such dramatic gains as those in the example are rarely possible (though they were if you played in internet-related stocks in the final two months of 1999). Think it through with lesser gains, ones which might perhaps appear more realistic in times when the market is firm, but not blazing away. Assume you buy a new issue which scores a 30pc premium in opening dealings, going from 100p to 130p, and taking your £1,000 investment to £1,300. In normal times, a 30pc gain over a few days is outstanding. If you hang on, hoping for a 40pc gain, the rise would be from 130p to 140p, and the value of the shares would go up from £1,300 to £1,400. Fine.

Assume, though, that you had sold, taken the 30pc gain, and re-invested the £1,300 cash. Assume that you picked a stock which went up by 10pc – after all, you held your first stock for a ten point gain from 130pc to 140pc of the original price. The 10pc gain on the re-invested £1,300 takes you up to £1,430 – which means you made £30 more, simply because you had more capital to play with by taking your opening gain. The sum is false, of course, because it ignores expenses.

It is worth thinking about if you are following an aggressive policy of chasing short-term profits. Many will say you should hold onto a winning stock for so long as it continues to rise. That is a view I broadly accept. Later, talking about selling shares, I return to this topic. Store away the idea of selling more quickly and re-investing, however. If you want to play aggressively, it makes sense. Make your own rules to suit your own temperament.

# SIX

# RIDING WITH THE DEALS

If you cannot get aboard a high-flying new issue just before take-off, you want a company which is going to be doing deals – any deals. Best of all, though, you want something which is going to undergo a radical transformation, hopefully by being used as a shell.

## Shell companies

The name gives a pretty good clue as to what shell companies are about. They are companies whose main asset is the share listing. If you buy control of one, you can save a certain amount of paperwork, and have a ready-made list of shareholders. The actual trading business has done badly, and has either been closed or sold, or is about to be. In effect, then, you have the empty shell of a company, waiting to have something popped inside it to revive it.

It is sometimes hard to see what the real advantage of popping anything worthwhile into a shell may be these days, since the Stock Exchange forces the new promoters to send out pretty much the equivalent to a flotation document which involves considerable expense. Sometimes it seems almost as easy to start afresh, floating on AIM or under the new techMark rules. Obviously there are times when those in control already have such an interest in the shell that it pays them to find something to keep it alive. And there are times when any tax losses in the old company might come in useful for the new one.

## Cash shells

What matters to shareholders – or prospective shareholders – is that there is action under way. The handiest shells of all are those which contain little but cash, with no untidy bits of old businesses to clutter the picture and perhaps deliver nasty surprises before they go – losses do have a habit of lingering on. Pure cash shells are frowned upon by the Exchange, which used to suspend the shares of any companies which had no trading business. In recent years, the attitude has become more sensible. With the advent of the Alternative Investment Market, a small band of entrepreneurs have begun creating cash shells, going through all of the business of getting a listing, and sitting there with companies which have little or no trading activity, and are simply searching for appropriate growth companies to buy.

Best-known of these is the "shell-meister" Michael Edelson, a director of Manchester United Football Club. He created a series of shells, all bearing the names of towns in the Manchester region, and popped a little sports business into them with the intention of buying it back out again when he found a real company. One became restaurant group Hartford, another sports rights agency Media Content. Most notorious of these is Knutsford. There was a similar operation by a group led by Damian Aspinall. One of their efforts became software group Keystone, and the other changed from Cambury to e-Capital. They, though, were hampered by an excessive number of warrants and options linked to the board. More successful was Grosmont, which the Vaughan brothers Oliver and Tom, have transformed into another internet incubator under the e-Vestment name.

At the time of writing, the longer-term success of these operations has yet to be established. That, though, is not what this game is about. All have been triumphant successes in delivering short-term capital gains. Knutsford shares have soared from 2 1/2p to over 250p, and e-Capital and e-Vestment multiplied ten-fold or more in the final months of 1999. Hartford has stuttered, but Media Content has begun to move nicely after a slow start.

What has sent the shares soaring is a combination of the names involved, and the industry they are moving into. Knutsford has depended purely and simply on the names and reputations of the four new players. The two "e" companies have taken off largely because they have moved into investing in young internet companies, the most fashionable area in the market. The association with names like artist Damien Hirst and publicist Matthew Freud has not been sufficient to pull Hartford higher. The restaurant business has been highly rated, but these boys already have a hint of yesterday's men about them, and have no record of business success. The City does not know them well, does not rate them. And the deal which put the first restaurant into the shell was done at an absurdly generous price to the vendors – so hard financial facts crept in there, outweighing the hype behind the names. Media Content also fizzled at first because the boys going in were largely unknown quantities, though they could claim a record of success in negotiating the exploitation of sporting rights in other businesses. They, too, sold their company in for what appeared to be an exotic rating, given the lack of a demonstrable ability to make money. Investors sat back to watch and wait.

Simply examining those few examples gives useful clues to what you want to see in shell companies. Obviously action – any action –is good. Shares in all of the cash shells moved ahead strongly before the key deals were announced. So getting in early is good. When the deals were known, the boys who had a strong record of making money were the ones who sent share prices soaring.

The Knutsford four – Archie Norman, Nigel Wray, Nick Leslau, and Julian Richer – were all known to the City, all proven deal-doers and money-makers. The record of the Vaughan brothers was not quite so well known, but they had prospered by building disco group Juliana's and selling to a big name. They had created Gander, a property company which was taken over. They had also been associated with other successful companies like Internet Technology Group and Redstone Telecom. They were money-makers, and were moving into the fashionable internet sector.

Cambury was restrained initially because the original board had overloaded the company with options and warrants which would heavily dilute the interests of anyone selling a successful business in. It stuttered because their earlier efforts, which created software company Keystone, got off to a poor start. Their record in quoted motor dealer Caverdale was also spotty. What made e-Capital workable was that they modified the terms of some of the options, moved into the hot internet sector, and effectively passed control to Hugh Osmond and his partner. They had gained a big reputation for doing exciting deals with Punch Taverns, and Osmond was one of the architects of the earlier terrific transformation of a tiny computer company into a massively successful restaurant group with the injection of the Pizza Express chain.

### *A tight market*

Ideally, then, what you want to see in a shell company is the injection of a business in a fashionable sector, engineered by businessmen with a proven record. Oh, and one thing more. We should not forget to toss in the magical ingredient which plays such a crucial role in sending new issues to the stars – a tight market in the shares.

Look at each and every one of these shell operations and you will find that the boys manage to tickle up the appetite of the market, and starve it of shares. At first glance, it may not appear so. Whenever a new bright new business is injected into a shell, the whole process is built around a fund-raising. It makes sense to start the new dream with debt cleared and cash in the bank. The idea is to build the new company, so that makes good sense.

Each time, the company going in is bought in exchange for shares in the shell. That gives the boys who own the new business a big stake in the continuing operation. They will want control. More important, they will want to be rewarded well. So they take shares at around the price at which trading was suspended. At that stage, the shell will have been valued at a few million pounds. The new enterprise will be much bigger, so the shell company issues tens, maybe hundreds, of millions of new shares to the vendors. When it returns to market, the enlarged company will be an altogether bigger, more attractive animal, with bright growth prospects. Or that, at least, is the idea. So shares in the expanded animal will start at a substantial premium.

It works wonderfully for everyone. The original investors see a big profit. The vendors of the business going in have oodles of shares, probably options galore, and are looking at a fat paper profit on their new shares – in effect, they may well have sold their business in for a generous price to start with. When trading begins in the new shares, they could find it valued at two or three times as much.

Along the way, extra shares will have been issued to provide adequate capital to the expanded company. Some of these may have gone to the vendors. You can bet your life a big chunk will have gone to assorted advisers and their acquaintances. And a smaller proportion will have been on offer to the original investors in the shell, with some more perhaps the subject of a placing to new investors.

Very few of these extra shares will be on sale in the short term. Because the injection will be close to offering a new company for sale, the boys who sold the business in will not be allowed to sell their shares – or many of them – for a year or more. And there may be an informal lock-in agreement with other investors among the advisers. Some who got stock in the placing may also understand that if they spoil things and dump too much of their stake in early dealings, they are unlikely to be invited to ride the next gravy train. So they will stick.

When trading resumes, and the general public gets a chance to invest in the new operation, there will be relatively few shares for anyone to buy, even though the size of the company might be very much greater. Thanks to the publicity surrounding the deal, punters will want in. The market-makers, effectively the share wholesalers who every broker has to use, will respond by pushing the price up sharply, hoping to tempt some sellers out (and to make a fat profit for themselves in the process, because they will have been given some stock in the placing at the low price). Fun and fat profits for all. Whoopee.

### *Issue arithmetic*

It is as well to keep a little simple arithmetic in mind when you are looking at these sort of operations. Small investors can get confused because they see shares trading at, say 48p, then an issue of new shares at, say, 10p. Suddenly the price falls.

In reality, it should mean no harm. It should be good news. A portion of the new shares is normally offered to old investors at the low price. This is either called a rights issue, or a claw-back. Either way, you should try to find cash to take up the new shares, if you can. You need to apply a little simple arithmetic, though, to understand the impact on the share price. If, say, the offer is of one new share at 10p for every four already held, and you take up the offer of new shares, you will have five where before you had four. Ahead of the issue, there were four at 48p – or a total value of 192p. Add one new share at 10p, and you have five at 202p. Divide that 202p by five, and you get a price of a fraction under 40 1/2p. That is the price you would expect the shares to fall to, all else being equal.

When they do that, they are marked as trading ex-rights, or ex-clawback, which means that anyone then buying the shares will not be entitled to the new 10p shares. For a while, rights to the new 10p shares will trade separately, and if you cannot afford to put up the 10p, you can sell the right to do that. You should get a good premium – in this example, around 30p a share. So you can alleviate any potential loss by selling the rights. Ask your broker. But do be alert. If you are not careful, and if you deal in a nominee account, you may not get the documents in time, and could miss out all round.

If you do not take up the new shares at 10p, or do not sell the rights, you have lost the potential profit on them. And you will have lost as your existing shares fall to 40 1/2p. If you buy the new shares at 10p, you lose nothing. You should gain, since in most cases, the shares will not fall all of the way to 40 1/2p, but might settle at, say, 42p.

### *Joining the fun*

It is wonderful if you were lucky enough or shrewd enough to buy in ahead of the action. But is it worth clambering aboard for the first time when the new business comes back to market ? It could be. Nothing in this book is set in stone. Moods and conditions change, and all investors should be constantly watching for those shifts in fashion, and ready to change tack with them. At the start of the New Millennium, it may well make sense to pile aboard early when dealings resume in shell operations, especially if they are internet-related. It may pay to buy anyway.

Think about it. The new boys, loaded down with shares, options, warrants and the dreams of their new shareholders, have gone in to make money – for themselves first, for anyone else would be nice if they can. Happily, their rewards are tied into the share price. Because they will have taken the main block of their shares at the pre-deal suspension price, they do not need it to rise further on resumption of dealings, if there is a hefty opening premium. Their profit is built in. But it is only a paper profit. They will not be able to realise it for a year, maybe more. Selling is always tricky for directors. Whatever the reason, it tends to depress the share price when they do it. So there is a natural tendency to hold on for as long as possible.

The share lock-in means, though, that they will be anxious that the price does not fall. The opening day profit only exists for them if they can sell at that level a year later. So there is a powerful incentive for them to work for shareholders for at least a year. Their advisers might have a similar lock-in. So they will be urging them to get it right, too.

The options and warrants they have given themselves – in some cases amounting to far larger sums than the value of the actual shares they hold – will depend upon share price levels. Study the document, and you will see what price the options can be exercised at, and when they can be exercised. This gives you a clue as to what targets the directors have to hit, the very minimum levels they will be seeking for the shares. This is why – obviously – if you are ever given the chance to vote on board options, you should see that they do set reasonably demanding price targets. Sadly, some recent deals allow directors to take up large chunks of extra capital with no terribly demanding target.

Generally, though the boys should be heavily motivated to keep the share price up in the first year or so, preferably to shift it much higher. They will be wanting to generate action, and do deals. Of course, that might be beyond their ability. Circumstances change, and some entrepreneurs manage only one lucky deal in their career. That is why the City places such a premium on backing those it knows, the directors with a proven record of money-making. There are no guarantees with them but the odds are better.

Keeping this in mind should offer a little reassurance to anyone contemplating buying into a revamped shell in early dealings. The board will want to build it, to sustain momentum. In many cases, they will have a plan of action mapped out. They are supposed to reveal it in the initial deal document if they have any clear plans already. That does not happen. Informally, though, a good team will have a pretty clear idea of the next deal or two, or three, when they do the first.

Back these boys, and you should be reasonably sure that you are going to see action. If nothing happens within three or four months, start worrying. Pester your broker, ask the company what is going on. If there is no deal inside six months, unless there are strong rumours of something afoot in the press, then sell. You might miss out, but better safe than sorry. The absence of an early deal almost certainly means something has gone wrong behind the scenes.

## *Takeover bids*

Shell companies are not the only ones which present money-making opportunities in the deal department. They are merely the most eye-catching and obvious way in which unexciting companies can be transformed into shares which are worth a gamble. The action you want might be sparked by a takeover bid, a merger, or the acquisition of a new subsidiary.

The best way to spot a possible takeover candidate is simply to read the financial press carefully. Bid rumours abound. Someone, somewhere, always knows about an impending bid, and talks or trades. Small wonder, given that there can be hundreds of City folk doing the paperwork required in a successful takeover.

Obviously the press is far from perfect in giving warning of bids. It probably predicts 400 out of every 52 successful bids. So do not deal on gossip alone.

There are a few clear clues. Obviously if someone starts building a share stake, the City wakes up to that pretty quickly. Anything above 14.9pc is serious, but anything above 3pc has to be declared, and is worth watching.

Look for shares which hold firm or rise on days when the market is falling, or doing nothing much. Any price which moves against the trend might be conveying a message of some sort. Check in something like Company Refs who the main shareholders might be. If they include two or more of the big boring investment houses who hold a stake in almost every one of the top 350 companies, there is a chance. People like fund manager PDFM have stumbled badly in the late nineties. Convinced for years that the market was set to crash, they have been building stakes in so-called "value" stocks, old-established companies with substantial assets. Because they have done so badly, they have been quietly encouraging bidders to talk to them about buying these stakes as the foundation for a bid. PDFM would welcome bid action simply because it peps up the prices of their dismal investments. Other institutions feel the same, though it is less obvious.

Be careful. While there are predators about, looking for companies they can break up, selling the assets piece by piece in the hope of establishing that the sum of the parts is greater than the price they paid for the whole (Philip Green did it brilliantly with Sears), they will not always pick the obvious targets. If nothing happens, you will be left with shares in a big, boring business going nowhere. It is an easy mistake to make. In my Daily Mail column, I tipped one-time textile giant Coats Viyella in the summer of 1999 because it looked so cheap for anyone with the nerve to bid and break it up – and it also had recovery potential. I told readers to sell a few months later at a loss of 11pc. Nothing had happened, and the price was drifting lower. It had looked very cheap, but was simply getting cheaper week by week.

There are a couple of lessons there. It is important not to hang about if your original idea looks wrong. So a stop loss is a good idea (more in the selling section of this book). Free the funds to move on into something more dynamic. And, though I was wrong, I had only recommended Coats Viyella because I thought that if no bidder appeared to exploit the asset backing, then the market would come to appreciate the trading recovery prospects. Two dreams were better than one. Sadly, neither survived a wake-up call from a dismal share price.

### *Market capitalisation*

Buy another book if you want all of the usual stuff about fundamental values – assets, market share, brand values and such. The more of them, the better, obviously. Be aware, though, that when you start getting into that sort of stuff – nothing wrong with it if you have the time and patience – you will merely be ploughing over old ground. Unless you are looking at a tasty tiddler, every broking and investment house in the City will have had an analyst looking at it, weighing it up. Because everyone will know about it, much of it will already be factored into the share price, so pleasant surprises will be few and far between. Watch the press for comments, or ask your broker. Or, these days, check the bulletin boards.

One crucial item, though, which often gets overlooked is the market capitalisation. This should probably have come up earlier and on many occasions in this book. It can be vital. The market cap, as it is often called, is simply what the company is worth by reference to the price of the shares. It is the company's stock market value.

Sometimes it can be quite hard to calculate, especially when you are looking at a business with warrants and such. Or perhaps different classes of shares. It appears in the price tables in The Financial Times on a Monday, though the figures are not always complete, because they do not take into account all classes of capital. Your broker should be able to help.

Market cap matters because it puts you in touch with reality pretty quickly and simply. Time and again, I find I use it as a starting point for looking at companies. It is particularly relevant in bids and deals. Time and again I have heard stories about Bloggs bidding for Jones, only to discover that the market cap of Bloggs is £9m, and Jones is valued at £54m. Such a deal is not impossible, but is unlikely. By the time Bloggs had paid the customary premium for control of Jones, it would need to make an offer worth, say, £65m. And the shares of a bidder generally fall. In normal circumstances, then, we would have had a company valued at £8m bidding for one worth £65m. It could happen, but the odds are against it.

Market cap comes in handy, too, when people begin spouting profit projections. A rise from £500,000 to £1.5m in profits sounds pretty good – unless you then realise that the company has a market value of £50m. Once again, that is not impossible. But is it less likely to mean that the prospective rise in profits will make much impact on the share price.

As a rough exercise, you can do a simple sum. Take profits of £1.5m, knock off 25pc for tax, and you have net profits, or earnings, of around £1.1m. If you divide that £1.1m into £50m, you get to around 45. That is the rough and ready pe, or price earnings ratio. And that is pretty steep, especially when you are talking prospective profits – profits people are forecasting for a year in the future. I know, by the way, that the sums are not too accurate. But they are in roughly the right area. I offer them as a simple way you can manage a reality check quickly, in your head. Sit down with the back of an envelope and work them through properly if you want to be more precise. But precision is not the point. All you are trying to do is make a quick judgement.

### *Bid tactics*

Bids are easy, if you own shares in any company which gets one. Sit tight, and accept the best bid at the last possible date. Bidders do tend to make an opening offer, and come through with a better deal later in the game. There are elaborate rules governing how bidders must behave, but in general, everyone must be treated alike. If you get nervous, you can always sell your shares in the market for instant cash, and then you have no worry about whether the bid will succeed or not.

Watch the financial press. That gives you the best idea of what is going on, whether there will be a counter-bid, whether the bidder will withdraw and walk away, letting the shares fall. Safety first is the rule. If you are in a company on the receiving end of a bid, you will have done nicely from the first move. Should anything make it possible that the bid will not go ahead, cut your risks and sell. Be especially careful about any hint of a Monopolies Commission reference. There is nothing like Government meddling to spoil the fun.

### *Acquisitions*

It is more difficult if you are aboard a company which is making a sizeable acquisition. You want the action, but you need to be sure that the board is getting it right. Usually, any significant acquisition will involve issuing many more shares. They might dilute your interest in the assets or profits of the company, and conventional investors will worry about that. A bolt-on business, expanding existing operations, may take time to bed down, and may cause a short-term profits hiccup. More immediately, however, there will be many more shares about, and many more potential sellers in the wings. So after a major acquisition, share prices often stutter for a spell. It will take a few supportive circulars from the company's broker, and a tour of big investors by board members, to sell the deal and settle doubts.

What the short term punter really wants is something which transforms prospects for the company. Anything which means a shift towards the internet is good, of course. Anything which brings in bright new management also helps.

Try to apply the sort of judgements covered elsewhere in this book. No matter how it is done, what everyone wants to see is evidence of more enterprising management taking the company into areas which might yield above-average growth.

# SEVEN

## *BLUE SKIES*

I love it. The great UK market feature of 1999 was the triumph of the techno-nerds. As the year rolled on, technology related stocks emerged ever more clearly as the market leaders. At one stage in December, it was calculated that the rise in the FTSE index of the top 100 shares, which ended the year up 18.2pc, was fuelled almost entirely by a small bunch of technology-related shares.

Look down the dismal list of conventional companies, and you can see why. Rentokil, Associated British Foods, Great Universal Stores, PowerGen, Boots, British American Tobacco, BAA and so on all lost out badly. Scan the top ten FTSE 100 performers, and the message is clear. Led by Colt Telecom, up 253pc, tech boys crowd the chart. Marconi, BSkyB, Telewest and Dixons are all there. Even advertising agency WPP joins in by virtue of the boom in internet-linked advertising. Microchip designer ARM Holdings is excluded only because it was not in the top 100 at the beginning of the year.

Spread the net wider, into the fields fished by smaller and more aggressive investors, and the top ten across the whole market is even more startling. Nine of them, as shown in The Daily Telegraph, are technology stocks entirely, most heavily internet-related. Leading the way with a rise of 7,600pc is Israeli internet systems company Geo Interactive Media. Then come Durlacher, Infobank, Recognition Systems, BATM, On-Line, Culver Holdings, eVestment, and E-Capital. The poorest performer, E-Capital, scored a gain on the year of 1,400 pc.

With the benefit of hindsight, it is easy to see where you should have been in 1999 – out among the tech stocks and the internet adventurers. In a way, it was an obvious self-fulfilling opportunity for many private investors. They were the ones who anticipated the action, rushed in and pushed the prices of some of these stocks ahead, and sucked in more small players as their enthusiasm spread.

By and large, the big institutions missed out. They are everywhere, of course. And in absolute terms, they made billions, while small punters made a few thousand here and there. In relative terms, though, while the institutions struggled to make gains of 20pc, small punters scored with 200pc gains and more. Even ARM only began to appear on the radar for big investors half-way through 1999. One or two institutions clocked on to Durlacher as it entered the FTSE 250 list in the autumn, but most were lamentably slow off the mark.

This is not merely another example of my routine self-indulgence – jeering at the big investors. There is rather more point to it. Small investors earned their gains by approaching investment with open minds. No doubt some succeeded simply because they got lucky, others because they did not know any better, and failed to understand that they were moving into what the traditionalists would dismiss as highly risky areas of the market. Above all, though, small investors triumphed in technology stocks because they were not hide-bound by investment convention.

His previous genius as an investor goes a long towards excusing Warren Buffett for a poor performance which saw shares in his Berkshire Hathaway flagship lose about a quarter of their value in 1999. It really is rather sad, though, to see him almost glorying in his inability to come to terms with technology stocks. His influence over investment thinking is so strong that implicitly condoning technophobia for share pickers is bad news for everyone.

For small investors ready to take a chance on quick profits from technology stocks, though, the Buffett story may have encouraging implications for the future. After a dismal year as "value investors"in 1999,more institutional investors will be buying into technology in the year 2000 and beyond, playing catch-up. Excellent news, that. The great danger of the 1999 boom was that the sector would run out of buyers. The greater fools – the last boys left holding the tin of inedible sardines – might be the big investors. With any luck, they will make money at buying tech stocks, and all will be well. In the short term, though, small investors must hope that the big money starts filtering down to smaller tech stocks. The chances are that it will.

Judging which ones to buy is extremely difficult. Readers of my Daily Mail Investment Extra column will know I was lucky enough to tip several high-flying tech stocks in 1999. I tipped Durlacher in March for an 18-fold gain by the end of the year. ARM was another of my tips (up nine-fold by the year-end). And E-Capital (tipped at 3 1/4p on October 30, up to 30p by December 31). Elsewhere I tipped eVestment. A year earlier, I recommended Geo, but advised readers to sell much too soon when it hit what proved to be temporary problems and the share price nose-dived.

The purpose of visiting a few of my greatest hits is not to boast (well, not entirely), but to try to demonstrate that I have some sort of record of success in this area. This is not a book written solely with the benefit of hindsight. Equally, it is not written with any great understanding of technology. Those who visited my www.michaelwalters.com web site during 1999 will have witnessed the odd quirks in presentation, and seen how badly I coped with what I am told are quite simple problems in using a word processor and the internet.

If I can stumble successfully through tipping technology stocks, you can too, I promise you. I am not proud of being a techno-clown. I do not spend sufficient time learning my way around. My time is occupied by tracking shares, keeping up with the market, and writing about it. Buffett's reluctance to invest in technology stocks because he does not understand how things work is misplaced. He does not need to understand it all. And punters looking to turn a quick profit in tech stocks certainly should not get discouraged by the complexity of the technology.

## *Bio-technology*

Among tech stocks, I most definitely include bio-technology companies. In many important ways, they are similar to the internet companies. They open a gateway to the great blue yonder, to the prospect of enormous rewards if all goes well. In many ways, though, they are easier to pin down. Any half-sensible bio-tech stock will be working in a particular area – a remedy for a certain type of cancer, a cure for Alzheimer's disease, a new method of delivering drugs. It will be possible to identify the value of that market, or something like it, and then form some sort of guess as to what success might mean.

Ask around. Talk to brokers, the company, anyone you can. Check the cash burn (how much the company spends each month), and set it against how much cash the company holds. The more cash the better, obviously. Especially since it will allow the company to negotiate better deals with parties interested in any new discoveries.

Individual bio-tech companies generally do not take their products to market. They rely on the giants with major distribution and marketing facilities. They sell the rights to promising discoveries, usually long before they are finally proven. Look to see what stage of development new products have reached. Pre-clinical is very early. If they go into phase one trials, that is helpful. Deals often start coming in at phase two, which means the chances of a commercial product have improved. Often the big boys will step in here, paying something up front to help fund the trials, and agreeing to milestone payments as research progresses. These sums can be substantial for small bio-tech companies. A move into phase three research generally indicates that the product has something like a 70pc chance of commercial success – very encouraging. Often it is easier to win regulatory approval to sell in Europe than in the USA. But the market is smaller.

After the British Biotech affair cast a shadow across the whole sector, bio-technology shares are beginning to make a come-back. Watch the sector. The nature of this business means it can generate big speculative gains – or losses.

### *Buying the dream*

What you are doing when you buy such stocks is buying the dream. That applies to almost everything I recommend. There are some more routine selections, but what I always try to do is to light on something which has the chance of delivering really exceptional growth if all goes well. That makes it almost obligatory to venture into areas which are hard to understand. If everyone knew about them, they would not offer exceptional opportunities. Debating which shares to tip for one week in November, I decided against recommending Carpetright, the excellent carpet retailing chain headed by Lord Harris. It is a company I had tipped successfully a couple of years earlier. A sensible contact suggested it was trading better than most people realised amid the retail gloom. It would have been relatively easy for me to confirm and to write a recommendation. In the end, I decided against it. The maximum potential gain I could see in Carpetright shares over a six month period was 25pc. In other times, that would have been more than enough. But in a market where tech stocks were exploding in price, the opportunity of gambling on a real high flyer was more appealing.

Ideally, I look for stocks which have a fairly predictable business to underpin the value, plus another venture which might just develop into something special, that magical glimpse of profits stretching beyond anything the market imagines. That happened when I recommended Internet Technology Group, a British internet service provider. As an isp, it looked reasonably valued, despite growing competition from Freeserve and others, and might just have a strategic position in the UK and Europe which could attract a US bidder. But the dream was a stake in GlobalWave, which owns the rights outside America for a microchip-based system which allows small charges to be made each time the viewer looks at individual pages on the net. That – and a whole bunch of allied possibilities – seemed to me to hold out great chances of growth, if it worked. And the basic isp business hedged the risk in Internet Technology shares, making it a near-perfect tip. In the event, a bid came in from America for Internet Technology.

It had worked nicely. Some of the upside was reflected in the bid price (shareholders were allowed to keep shares in a company which owned the GlobalWave operation), and the predictable value for the isp activities had covered one of the basic rules from the beginning of this book – limit the downside.

### *Evaluating the new stuff*

Much of the fun in the second half of 1999 was in internet-linked stocks. Despite the predictable howls of warning from the doomsters who have missed out and are reluctant to admit it, that could continue well into 2000, maybe longer. Evaluating net stocks, though, is tough. Especially if you are accustomed to conventional analytical tools. Most net companies are suffering losses, have no significant assets, are headed by relatively inexperienced directors, and cannot establish the extent of the market they are shooting at. In that situation, how do you tell the good from the bad?

No-one can. They are all guessing. The internet boom has tossed away all established measures of what the City imagines to be value. Forgive me if I do not hunt about for the correct figures, but how can you talk about real value when you have US companies capitalised at £3bn losing hundreds of millions of pounds a year – and set to go on losing big money for some time to come ? Read any of the hide-bound pundits as they churn out columns knocking it all. They have time enough to research the statistics. We all know the big picture. The establishment sees it as black, but the more adventurous investors and especially small-time speculators see it as golden.

So it is. For a while, at least. The trick is not to be caught holding the parcel when the music stops. It will not stop for all of the net companies. Everyone agrees that some will go on to be giants, massively profitable. Many will flop. But if you are not a big investor, bound to pick a stock and stick with it, it scarcely matters. Get aboard while the going is good, jump off with as much profit as you can when it begins to falter.

### *Phoney figures*

There have been several attempts at rationalising what is going on. For the moment, I cannot quite remember them. Analysts assign a value per head for each subscriber to each internet service. If one company's subscribers are valued at £1,400 each by dividing the number of subscribers into the company's market value, does that make such a company dearer or cheaper than one whose subscribers are valued at £1,000 apiece?

Who knows? So far, the figures are phoney. Until they come close to being translated into sustainable profits of some sort, it is an empty game. Even the business of claiming that if NICKIT.com has a greater market share than BLAGGER.com, then NICKIT is worth more is distinctly dubious. We are all out there in the middle of the ocean, struggling to find a rock we can stand on. Yet everything around us is shifting all of the time. Who knows whether these subscribers (in most instances subscribers who simply sign on and do not actually pay a penny of revenue to the company) are worth anything at all? In the end, someone has to sell them something, to generate profit from them in some way. And when it comes to market share, it is impossible to know the size of any market we are shooting at. Next week someone may come up with a new internet idea which changes the whole frame of reference, and steals it all away.

### *What they are worth*

Sorry about this, but in the end, it comes down to accepting that shares in internet companies are worth what someone will pay for them. The whole business is still in its infancy, and it is not sensible to ascribe firm values to anything.

If some institutions like to swap vanities with each other and pretend they have devised a system for attaching firm values to what is beyond rational valuation, so be it. That does give some temporary measure of worth for those who believe it. If it makes NICKIT.com worth 50pc more than BLAGGER.com, then there is a frame of reference for a while between those who believe in it.

### *Common sense criteria*

Right now, the internet is at the heart of all such action. But the basic principles apply more widely, to all new areas. This is where the City establishment and their conservative approach to investment falls down. The shock of the new is too great to take. Be it internet, telecoms, bio-tec, or some other exciting new areas of opportunity which we do not yet know about, these are sectors which cannot be judged by established criteria. You have to be brave, take a great deal on trust, make what judgements you can, and hope for the best. You have to gamble.

It is almost embarrassingly obvious to say it, but because these are areas in their infancy, they have no history. There is no set of accepted values by which to judge them. Everyone is guessing. Those who slam share values because they relate to untried technology are as foolish as those who try to set an eventual target for the value of such ventures. They may be overvalued because they may prove not to have a viable future. But because they involve pushing into new frontiers, we cannot put a cap on the likely value. We simply do not know what is yet to be discovered, how they might develop.

This is not to suggest that all attempts at research and assigning value are nonsense. The more you understand the science, the technology, the better placed you should be to judge whether it could work or not. So the big investors have an advantage, in that they can afford to invest in those who have such skills. That is why something like the biotechnology trusts associated with the Rothschilds make sense. They are run by managers and scientists.

It takes a while, though, for the big boys to wake up to the opportunities, to persuade themselves that they should bother with learning about the new. So they are generally slow into new areas. Small investors who can develop a feel for what is going on – with imperfect understanding – may do just as well, better perhaps, because they have open minds. And in investment terms, there are certain simple rules which help swing the odds in your favour. They apply to almost any investment – and more acutely to today's latest fashion, whatever it may be.

What we are looking at is a collection of common sense criteria, such as –

1. The reputation of the directors, and their record in the industry, and for making money
2. The reputation of the advisers, and their ability to make money
3. Deals with established companies
4. The size of any fund-raising
5. The plausibility of the business plan
6. The extent of the competition
7. The market capitalisation of the whole company
8. The number of shares freely available in the market
9. The share options and other incentives in place for the directors
10. The market fashion
11. The company's market profile

No great mystery about that lot, is there? You and I, and anyone else with half a brain could make some sort of sense of those measures. No rocket scientists need apply.

We have discussed most of these factors in earlier chapters. They are simple notions which apply pretty much universally in assessing investments. There is not a great deal more to say. Reputation is what has sent punters piling in to New Media Spark and almost anything associated with Luke Johnson, who has proved himself remarkably astute – though not infallible – as a company promoter and deal-doer over the past five years. The arrival of Hugh Osmond helped transform the rating of e-Capital, and so on.

It is worth drawing special attention on item two to the growing reputation of Durlacher, the broking business which chairman Geoffrey Chamberlain and back-room brains David Tabizel have transformed from a third-rate stockbroking business into the largest centre in Europe of knowledge about the internet and related industries. That has sent Durlacher shares soaring, and had a snowball effect. The more internet deals the house does, the more it learns. And the more it learns, the more internet ideas it attracts. So Durlacher's involvement in any UK tech issue means it has the best of pedigrees, and a better-than-average (though as yet unproven) chance of success. That means any deal associated with Durlacher is likely to attract a handsome premium. It has allowed them to bring in some heavy friends. The blue-blood broking house of Cazenove handled the flotation of 365 Group, a company created by the Durlacher team.

Elsewhere among advisers, a more conventional pecking order applies. When it was wrongly reported that US giant Goldman Sachs was behind the pre-Christmas fund-raising at eVestment, the shares leapt. In fact, a couple of former Goldman boys are involved – good, but not quite so good. And so it goes.

It is always worth reading the flotation or deal document, if you can get hold of one. If it mentions deals or links with other companies, particularly established big names, that is obviously encouraging. What you are looking for is endorsement by association – a sign that someone else in the industry thinks the new company has something worth supporting.

The amount of money being raised is obviously important. The more the better, on one level. Yet you do not want to see so much that the market is flooded with shares. That brings in item eight, the free float. So long as the directors, advisers and their associates take up stock and agree to hold it for a spell, the going should be fairly good.

Measuring the plausibility of the business plan is altogether trickier. No-one can be sure about anything, yet applying common sense does not go amiss. Obviously you should check to see if there is a mass of competition, and try to establish how well-established, well-financed, and powerful that competition may be. If you are looking at someone with a scheme for selling cut-price cds over the net, and they are planning to compete with the US giant Amazon.com, you may have doubts about the viability of the scheme. On the other hand, a company called Medi@invest caught my eye at the end of October when it announced that it planned to take a large stake in an internet service provider aimed exclusively at children, with the support of several well-known characters. At that point, given that Medi@invest was capitalised at under £10m and there were no obvious competitors up and running, the business plan looked pretty plausible. It might not succeed, but catching them while they were young made obvious sense.

### *Keeping small*

Part of the reason for gambling on Medi@invest at that stage lay in the relatively small value of the business. Traditionalists will suggest that a price tag of almost £10m for a new company entering an untried market with a new product was quite pricey enough. Yet by internet standards, that was not so. Other net players with less obviously appealing ideas were valued at £100m or more. Medi@invest was being backed by stockbroker Mike Whitaker, former head of Collins Stewart, one of the livelier brokers, Whitaker himself had links with other internet players, and the presence of a half-decent broker known for supporting smaller companies suggested that the real downside was modest – at that stage. Investors were then beginning to develop an appetite and appreciation for small net-linked companies. Medi@invest might not look pure magic, but it was still unproven, and the market mood was such as to give new net companies the benefit of the doubt. Who could be sure what would come next?

Looking at the business plan, it is worth paying particular attention to potential sources of revenue. It is remarkable that these almost appear as an incidental to some grand and glorious plans. Many companies are pinning their hopes on advertisers. But as internet ideas proliferate, competition for cash from advertisers is getting ever rougher. So be careful.

It is even more dangerous to find a company relying for a chunk of revenue on sharing the cost of telephone calls. Part of the original Freeserve model, which offered internet services free, depended on splitting the revenue generated by people dialling up the service. That has become common-place, and with the arrival of companies offering free calls, and against a background of falling net phone charges from BT and the other telecoms companies, it is a less reliable source of revenue.

Fascinating and instructive to look at the strategy statement for Internet Indirect, the net-related fund headed by Mark Slater, supported by an impressively experienced board. Talking about minimising the risks attached to their prospective investments, they say they are sceptical about business plans which envisage multi-year losses, which aggressively subsidise customers, or which are overly dependent on future advertising revenues. The company will focus on areas such as media content, software, enabling technologies, e-commerce and internet infrastructure, including wireless, where barriers to entry and a degree of specialisation provide a reasonably rapid transition to profitability. It all makes eminent sense, a lesson for all net investors.

The size of the companies is important. While they are small, it is easy to believe they have room to grow. When you could spot a potential player with a market capitalisation of under £10m, it hardly seemed worth selling. Never mind the slim asset base and lack of profits. Look at the bright blue sky. As more and more little internet stocks began to fly, size became less important. As one stock reached a market capitalisation of £30m, it made others in the sector look more reasonable at £20m, even if they had practically nothing. Then came the £100m internet infant, and suddenly the £30m stocks did not seem so expensive. So the sector began to get ratcheted up.

What qualifies as "small" in this context is hard to say. It keeps changing. Small is beautiful for private investors in the early days. Market value of £10m or less is fine, but anything over £100m is much more questionable. Suddenly you have a half-serious stock which either has a lot of shares in the market, and many potential sellers if things go wrong. Or you have a stock where punters are sitting on profits which are not just fat, but super-fat, and all the more tempting to take if any hint of trouble appears.

Be sure of one thing. When you are gambling in internet stocks, you are playing in a particularly volatile game. When prices turn, they are liable to turn far and fast. Market-makers will not hesitate to slam prices in the face of relatively light selling. At times, that will create a buying opportunity. That happened briefly in November. But in just two dodgy days, many small punters suffered sharp losses. Nerves were really tested. In the event, buyers came in quickly, and most stock bounced back up. But that will not always be the way. So stay near the door – and pay special attention to the chapter on selling. Enjoy the net boom while it lasts. It will not last forever.

### *Internet incubators*

Much of the excitement among small new stocks has been stoked up around the so-called incubator funds. Perish the thought, but these are rather like investment trusts – they raise money from the public by issuing shares, and use that money to buy into other companies. The net incubators aim to finance new or relatively new internet companies before they come to market. Details vary, but broadly speaking, they aim to benefit from buying into unquoted companies relatively cheaply, selling for much higher valuations when they float. Most expect to take stakes in between ten and twenty companies.

To my mind, the incubators are a safer bet than individual internet enterprises. They are managed by individuals who develop some degree of skill in sorting good ideas from bad – they all get so many approaches for money that even the most inexperienced fund manager soon begins to learn. So the incubator investor ought to benefit from that skill. The funds also offer a good spread of risk. One or two duds in a list of twenty are unlikely to prove catastrophic. And they benefit from the very big valuations accorded any new net companies which have made their way to market. So one good investment could multiply three or four-fold in the run-up to flotation, then multiply by ten-fold as the market chases the shares higher in early dealings. The rewards for getting one investment right are potentially enormous, while the downside attached to mistakes is fairly modest.

Traditionalists have ignored this, and have fussed over the gap between the value of the investments – or cash – in the funds, and the market capitalisation of the fund. In many cases, these shares have rushed ahead, to stand at three, four or more times the value of their assets.

Never mind. So long as the companies do not get too big, it matters little. At the end of 1999, a clear pattern was emerging. Each company would exploit the inflated share price to raise more cash at around the higher share value, thus automatically raising asset value, and reducing the gap between asset value and market value. Take a simple example. Say SUPERNUTS.com has shares selling at 32p, to give it a market value of £32m, against an asset value of £8m, or 8p a share. In order to raise asset value to market capitalisation, the manager has to achieve four-fold growth in his portfolio. But if SUPERNUTS.com then raises £8m by issuing more shares at the market price, the market value of the company rises to £40m, and the net asset value to £16m. So the manager has to get an uplift of only 2 1/2 times – not so difficult in this climate. And he has more fire power to play in bigger deals.

Watch what happens. This pattern is likely to recur among internet funds, levering themselves up by their own bootstraps. Along the way, they will begin bringing in bigger investors, the institutions who missed out on the early excitement. They are being quietly kicked by sales managers who want to be able to tell the world that they have funds in the market hot spots. They will know from press comments, and probably their own personal share trading, that the fun and games have been in the infant internet sector, and will want to get a piece of the action. They will lack the skills or the nerve to pick internet stocks for themselves, and will try to play safe by backing the incubator funds.

At first, they will go for the names they know. That is why New Media Spark quickly rocketed to a market value of over £200m. Fund managers knew Luke Johnson was aboard, and understood he has a knack of delivering the goods. So they backed him. As they grow more confident, they will put cash into the smaller funds. That, in turn, will give those smaller funds more scope. It will bring in powerful investors with the cash and inclination to invest alongside the incubators in some companies before they come to market. This extra muscle will strengthen those companies, making them all the more attractive and rewarding for the incubator funds. In theory, at least, it forms a virtuous circle.

Sorry if this sounds like a load of waffle. In reality, it outlines the case for backing the incubators, and explains how to tell if they might be getting it right. I say "might" because no-one really knows how far and fast the internet boys will actually go, when they might start making profits. Remember – everyone is guessing.

# EIGHT

# *LIVING AND DYING IN THE MARKET*

Sometimes, it seems, picking the right stock is only part of the battle. Coping with the quirks and complications of the various markets, and the dealing dodges all around can cause quite a headache. In reality, though, differences between markets do not matter that much, so long as you are on a winner.

Though it dances to the tune of the big investors, and pays only lip service to the private client, the London Stock Exchange is the best bet for most purposes. Shares with a full listing in London are probably the most straightforward to deal in. Though there is no guarantee that you will be able to buy or sell freely in all shares at all times, this market does better than most. It is reasonably well-regulated, and information is gathered and circulated pretty widely. And shares in UK companies with a full listing can be bought and sold in a tax-saving Personal Equity Plan, if you were fortunate enough to set one up while they were still valid, or an ISA now.

## *AIM*

The Alternative Investment Market requires less stringent qualifications for companies seeking a quotation. It was set up to encourage smaller, newer companies to come to market. In theory, the trading record needed to be shorter (some start-ups are allowed), relatively few shares needed to be placed in the market, and costs were intended to be much smaller. In practice, charges have mushroomed, and are now almost as great as for a full listing. In general, it may not be possible to buy and sell freely in such large volumes of shares as on the full market, partly because the free float is small to start with. Much, though, depends on the nature of the company. Because it is a junior market, and is largely composed of younger, smaller companies, and liquidity can be limited, AIM attracts less buying by big institutions. As a result, the stocks are less thoroughly researched. It may be possible to spot good opportunities before the big boys see them. Many of the internet sensations are traded on AIM. Sadly, it is not possible to put such stocks in a PEP or ISA and shelter them from gains tax.

## *techMARK*

Worried that it was losing ground to other exchanges – the prime motive for any new initiative from the London Exchange over many years – the Stock Exchange introduced something called techMARK in November 1999. Initially, it simply lumped together more than 170 technology companies which were already quoted, and slapped a techMARK banner on them. This re-branding exercise worked to remarkable effect, and the majority of the shares which were pulled in have risen strongly. It helped draw attention to the technology content in several businesses which had been neglected, and the whole lot attracted buyers as managers set up specialist funds to channel money into the new sector.

In theory, there are new listing rules which make it easier for technology companies to gain a share listing, and issue shares. The companies will not need a three year trading record (the AIM qualification), but will be required to report quarterly, with a minimum value of £50m on flotation. At least 25pc of the shares must be made available on a free float. Companies have been allowed to apply to join techMARK, so it is worth watching for such plans, given the initial favourable impact on share prices.

## *OFEX*

Founder John Jenkins tends to argue when Ofex is called a less regulated market outside the Stock Exchange. He likes to call it a trading facility. There are shares in several hundred companies available on Ofex, and many of them rely on matching buyers with sellers. That means it is not possible to trade freely in many of the Ofex shares. You can wait for months before you can find a buyer– even then, one might not appear, especially at anything like the price at which they traded earlier.

On the other hand, some Ofex companies are quite busy. J.P. Jenkins, the firm which created and runs Ofex, does match buyers and sellers.

And some companies have established stockbroking firms standing behind them, effectively making a market. So the better companies might trade tens of thousands of shares each day on most days.

Because admission to the Ofex facility costs only a few thousand pounds, assuming the company passes a vetting committee which tries to ensure reasonable standards, it is seen as a useful way to raise modest amounts of risk capital. It can act as a stepping stone to AIM or a full listing. A few highly successful companies have made the transition. If you can spot good businesses early, you can buy on Ofex in the early days, and do very well. But Ofex companies in general are smaller, weaker, and much riskier than those traded on the London Stock Exchange. Some do disappear without trace if Jenkins kicks them out because they do not meet his rules.

The facility is supported by an excellent web site – www.Ofex.co.uk – which gives real time prices. It also gives access to Newstrack, an information service which carries announcements profiles and basic data on all Ofex companies, plus any announcements. Until you learn your way around, it is best to steer clear of Ofex, given the trading uncertainties. But as you become more comfortable with share gambling, Ofex is worth investigation.

## *Easdaq*

Easdaq is a relatively new pan-European share market, based in Belgium, and with the stated intention of catering for international growth companies. The dream was that it would attract potential high-flyers, and present them to European, UK and American traders. It has been a damp squib. Several interesting companies have listed on Easdaq, but have been disappointed at the lack of trading in their shares, and poor liquidity in the market.

While prices are available freely on a web site – www.Easdaq.be – many British brokers are barely aware that the market exists, and will shy away from transacting deals. It can be hard to track announcements from Easdaq companies, and share prices do not always respond to information. There are also additional dealing costs – there is a charge for share custody – which act as a further disincentive.

That said, such problems sometimes create an opportunity. Autonomy, the excellent British intelligent internet search engine company, is traded there, and has often been reckoned undervalued as a result. I tipped Antisoma, a British drug company which was traded there. Even when Antisoma clinched a brilliant contract, news of it took so long to be reflected in the Easdaq price that it presented a wonderful buying opportunity for alert UK investors. It is not worth wasting much time or effort on Easdaq, but every now and then...

## *Nasdaq*

Few will have escaped the overblown and expensive ads for Nasdaq on British TV. This is second in the US share market ranking, behind the New York Stock Exchange and ahead of the American Stock Exchange. It does list some brilliant companies – and many more tiny, half-dead ones. Because it features many technology stocks, and they attract a bigger following and higher rating in the US, a Nasdaq listing is the goal for many young, enterprising British companies. Some gain a dual listing – London and Nasdaq – and that does help the share rating.

Few small punters will want to venture into buying shares directly on Nasdaq. The problem of tracking news and prices is too great, though increasingly the US broking houses which operate in the UK do offer the facility to trade on Nasdaq.

## *ADRs*

One particular warning, though, when you do come across a company with a dual listing. British shares in the US are frequently traded as American Depositary Receipts. What really matters about them is that one ADR tends to bundle together three or four of the British shares. So if you see a share at 60p in the UK, do not get excited if you see it trading at $4 in the US. That $4 will be the equivalent to 240p (using an exchange rate of 60p to the dollar). But it will be the price for a bundle of four of the UK shares.

### *Market size*

Sorting equities from your ADRs may not trouble too many short term share punters, but market size is certainly something to keep an eye on whatever market you are using. It should play quite a part in determining how many shares you buy in the stock you fancy. Basically, brokers do not own the shares they buy for you, and do not take up the shares you sell. They go to a market-maker, effectively a wholesaler in shares. He undertakes to buy and sell those shares at prices he posts on a screen available to all brokers. He also undertakes to buy or sell at that price in particular quantities.

Always check the normal dealing size in any share you fancy before you buy. Be careful not to buy more than are readily available. In theory, there are at least two market-makers in each stock. In the big companies, there can be a dozen. If each one is offering to deal in, say, 10,000 shares, then using all 12 market-makers, it ought to be possible to buy or sell freely in 120,000 shares of that company at a time. In practice, of course, that does not work. Market-makers follow each other. When one changes a price, the others may follow suit without actually trading. Frequently there is one market-maker who sets the pattern for the rest. Again in big stocks, there may be two or three lead market-makers, including perhaps those whose firms also act as financial advisers – behind a Chinese Wall with allows no information to pass from one function to another. You do believe that, don't you? In smaller stocks, there may effectively be only one market-maker. Others may be there in theory, but quoting silly sizes at poor prices.

### *The spread*

Market-makers do make profits by buying at one price and selling at another, effectively gambling in the shares. Most of their profit, though comes from the spread between the price at which they will buy (the bid price), and sell (the offer price). Different market-makers may quote different buy-sell spreads for the same share. The less active the market, the wider the spread. And if the market-maker does not want to deal, or prices are moving fast, he might widen the spread. That can hurt, especially in low-value stocks. Whereas a leading share might be quoted at, say, 299p to 301p and be tradeable in large volumes, a less popular stock might be called 295p to 305p. Or even 290p to 310p. Or worse. All though, have a mid-price of 300p.

The spread can be a killer, especially in penny stocks. At one extreme, you might get a mid-price of 1 1/2p (the price the papers quote), and find the real price is 1 1/4p to sell, 1 3/4p to buy, a massive gap. And if you buy at 1 3/4p, and the price eases slightly, the next quote could be 1p to 1 1/2p. In one change, the share bought at 1 3/4p can only be sold for 1p – a massive setback.

In practice, a good broker should be able to deal inside those prices, trading on a buy-sell spread of perhaps 1/8p or 1/4p. But the spread, every bit as much as trading uncertainties, is what can make gambling in very low-priced shares such a risky game. And the market-maker can widen the spread without warning. It would not be too unusual to find your share at 1 1/4p to 1 3/4p suddenly being quoted at 1p to 1 3/4p if the market-maker felt nervous. Always check the spread with your broker before trading, and be especially careful about buying large quantities of shares which have a big spread.

### *The touch*

If you have a decent broker, and one you can talk to, he will automatically check the "touch" for you, and deal on it. The touch comes when different market-makers quote different price spreads for the same share, and is made up by combining the two closest prices – effectively the best deal available. So if one broker is calling a share 220p to 225p, and another is quoted 222p to 227p,the touch will be 222p (the best bid price) to 225p (the best offer) – a 3p spread instead of 5p.

### *Thin markets*

Where there are several market-makers, or a couple who deal readily in fair quantities at sensible prices, you have what is called a liquid market. An illiquid – or thin - market, naturally, is quite the opposite. That can be an advantage when prices are rising. The market-maker will shift the quotation up quickly to encourage investors to sell shares to him so that he can meet buying orders. He may also raise prices sharply to attract sellers, sometimes to obtain shares he has sold in advance. Or he could do quite the opposite. If he has sold shares he does not own – is "short" in market parlance – he might mark prices down sharply, hoping to scare speculative traders into selling, thinking something is wrong.

If there really is bad news, prices can be marked down sharply before anyone sells a single share. That is why it is important to check market size before you trade. You may not be able to cover yourself entirely, but if you have taken a chance and bought twice as many shares as the market-maker will normally trade in, you risk getting hammered very hard. You will be faced with a lower price for the normal quantity, and a still lower price for the rest. Or you might find that there is suddenly no market at all – you cannot sell at any price, or can shift only a very small number. That can mean wipe-out.

### *SETS*

You might come across the Stock Exchange Automated Trading System, or SETS. This only applies to the top 120 or so shares, though the number is slowly expanding. It is an automated system, with computers matching buyers and sellers, cutting the market-makers margin. It is imperfect, leads to totally daft prices being recorded from time to time, and runs alongside a conventional market-making book in the same stocks. It will rarely bother you, and is really most relevant to the big boys. The Exchange is talking about expanding a similar system to the top 250 shares, adding a layer of complication.

### *Bulletin Board*

Some fully-listed shares are tough to trade. No-one wants to deal in them much. These are listed on what is called SEATS, or the Bulletin Board. They both come close to a matched bargains system, where you can only buy or sell if there is a corresponding seller or buyer, though the SEATS system does have one market-maker involved. In general, you should avoid trading in shares with such a sorry market, unless you are absolutely 100pc sure you are on a winner – and no-one can really be that sure.

## *Trading volumes*

Keeping an eye on market size is always a sensible discipline. It also tends to prevent you from becoming over-committed to any one stock. Concentrating your efforts is fine, but putting all of your eggs in one basket is dangerous. Trading volumes in listed stocks are available. Your broker can tell you, and some internet services might provide them. In AIM stocks, it is trickier. They are reported after a delay. You cannot tell how many shares have been traded on the day you play. If you want to get really serious, you will check what sort of trading levels are representative, and be careful to keep inside them when you buy.

There is also a clue to direction, of course. If shares rise sharply on small trading volumes, that is less encouraging than a similar rise on a day when there has been big business.

## *Sell on a rising market*

There is no set guide to share trading, but the safest way to a quick profit is to sell when you least fancy it – on a rising market. Headlines which talk of a soaring market, or a crash, always tell only a part of the story. For every buyer, there must be a seller. For anyone to sell, there must be someone to buy. Though it may break your heart not to try to squeeze the last penny of profit out of a winning trade, it might be best to sell when there are still buyers clamouring for stock. And to try to buy on a dull day, when there may be more sellers. The essence of successful trading is anticipation. You want to move before the herd.

## *The falling sword*

It is trickiest, of course, to time buying on a dull day. There is an old market cliché about never trying to catch a falling sword. It makes some sense, since up or down, market moves tend to be over-exaggerated

If you buy before a price has stopped falling, you might be surprised how much further it falls. That counts. Losing money is painful, and if you buy a share which does not rally, then you could quickly be faced with the possibility of having to sell at a loss simply to save a reasonable proportion of your capital. If you buy a little late, pay a few pence more than you might have done by being brave, you are not so much exposed to risk. All being well, you have only lost a little profit, not jeopardised stake money.

### *Danger signals*

While we are tackling ancient market lore, it might be as well to trot through a few more of the old clichés, the classic signs that should make you think twice about investing in a particular company. Hackneyed some of them may be, but it is surprising how often they turn out to make sense

Beware the boss who –

Takes more than one other directorship, joins a Government committee, is active in the CBI or the City.
Tells the press his shares are cheap
Opens a head office in Mayfair
Wins a press award as man of the year
Drives a Rolls-Royce or Bentley with personalised number plates
Is honoured for services to industry
Boasts new offices opened by the Prime Minister
Is pictured in the annual report alighting from a helicopter
Opens an office in China
Appears in more than two pictures in the staff magazine
Is photographed in soft focus for the annual report
Calls shareholder meeting at Christmas or on New Year's Eve
Owns a massive yacht
Joins the board of a football club
Appears frequently in the gossip columns
Plays polo
Recruits a Royal to the board
Leaves the audit account with a local firm

# THE INFORMATION AND THE INTERNET

Reading a book like this is all very well if you want to get into the share gambling game. But when you actually get down to doing it, you need a sensible broker and access to decent sources of information. The two do not necessarily go together. Above all, you need to get on the internet.

Sorry about that. You can trade shares perfectly happily without being on the net, but all of a sudden, it puts you at a significant disadvantage. There really is an information revolution in progress. It has gathered pace over the past couple of years. In 1999, it began to explode.

The internet influences your trading opportunities in two crucial ways – it gives you virtually instant access, and it allows you to tap into an almost infinite range of information.

Instant access might sound a touch daunting. No-one wants to feel chained to a computer screen all day, watching their shares in case something happens. That, though, helps give City professionals a big advantage. They are there, all hours of the day, sitting in front of several screens, ready to react the instant any news breaks. There is an enormous cost to companies who employ these people. The fact that they consider it essential gives you an indication of how well it pays off.

In the past, private investors have been at a massive disadvantage, trading on second and third-hand information, coming in days after the market has seen, absorbed and interpreted any developments. Read the morning papers and you are getting distinctly dated stuff, yesterday's news. Every investment house has experts who have tried to anticipate any development, and have a strategy in hand, ready to react immediately to whatever variation occurs. Share prices have always reacted instantly to news. In the past, only the professionals were in a position to take advantage of this. The internet tilts the playing field a little, gives the alert private investor the chance of learning what is happening almost as quickly as anyone in the market.

In practice, even with the internet, the private investor will not be able to react as quickly as the City. It will not always make a great deal of difference. But the net offers individuals the option of getting into the action pretty quickly, should they choose. Even if you do not want to track your investments all through the day, you will find it better to be able to catch up with the news in the evening, think about it, and be ready to go on the next morning, if you choose.

You can also get the raw data, the unfiltered news. If you have access to a news service on the net, the full announcement is the one bearing the RNS (regulatory news service) tag. That usually carries phone numbers for the company (which may not welcome the call while the press and analysts are trying to get through) and the public relations agency. The AFX version, widely reported, comes through a news agency. When you rely on the press, you cannot be sure your company's action will have been reported. It is unlikely to be reported in full, and it will usually be subjected to an element of interpretation. As a financial journalist for nearly forty years, I know what happens. No-one misleads intentionally, but so-called facts can be presented to fit a particular view. And even in selecting what to put in and what to leave out (can you imagine how hard it is to condense a four page statement into 100 words, at speed, and still make sense?), journalists add their own slant unintentionally.

### *Price changes*

Should you get the chance to watch trading screens for several hours, you might be surprised how often and dramatically prices can change. Though tracking end of day changes might suggest nothing much has happened, that can conceal big moves, up in the morning, down in the afternoon. Sometimes a minute can mean a great deal of money. Few will want, or be able, to track prices by the minute. But the internet does offer that opportunity. More important, it lets you look in now and then, when you have the chance. For short term traders, that can make all the difference. Remember, if you are holding 10,000 shares in something, a rise of 1p means a gain of £100. That is a lot for the £1,000 share punter.

## Information overload

The internet might be even more valuable for the information it brings to your fingertips. In truth, there is too much, information overload. You could spend every hour of the day surfing the net, uncovering fascinating new facts about almost anything. Already the volume of investment information is enormous, far too much for anyone to take in. Much of it is of dubious quality, but there is more than enough good stuff.

Several services offer real time share prices, and instant access to all company announcements, either summarised or in the full form as filed with the Stock Exchange. As I write, almost all of the real time price services require you to pay a monthly subscription fee, or something else. There are a few free ones, but I have not tested them myself, and it seems that several of them can get overloaded, or have other disadvantages. That will change. Before too long, you will be able to get most of what you want easily and cheaply, if not completely free.

There are many other free sites which offer a general service, the on-line equivalent to a daily paper, with news, features, statistics, columnists and so on. And there are a variety of sites on which investors can swap ideas. They are fascinating, addictive, and often highly informative.

## Going on-line

Ideally, you need the net. If you have managed to find £1,000 so that you can play the market, use it instead to get on the net. If nothing else, it will be invaluable for equipping your children to cope with life. They are going to need computer skills, and their potential and earning power will suffer without them.

Do not be intimated by the technology. I am a computer klutz. I understand very little about the technology of computers and the net, but using their power has transformed my life and earning ability. All you need is a half-decent computer, a modem, and a telephone line. The modem links your phone to the computer and brings access to the internet. Any computer shop will supply all you need, and tell you how to do it. Hooking it up will be frustrating, unless (like me) you have a teenager who still knows everything. If you are worried, it is worth buying from a store which will send someone to connect it all for you. Believe me, that is a service worth paying for.

Once you have your internet access up and running, learn your way around it. And begin saving another £1,000 so you can play the market.

### *Choosing a stockbroker*

After encouraging everyone to get onto the internet, it might come as a surprise to suggest that you will be better off buying and selling shares through a traditional broker. In a way, I am cheating when I give such advice. I have not tried to trade on-line, over the internet, and do not use an execution-only broker. So while most of this book draws on years of experience, this section does not.

To my mind, there is no substitute for developing a good relationship with an individual broker. This is not easy, especially at times when markets are active. They are too busy to take on new clients, and it takes time to develop a sensible relationship. If you are outside London, you might have more luck with a local broker. They still exist. If you are very lucky, you might find a small branch office of one of the big boys, staffed by an old-timer who prefers to work nearer his home, under less pressure. No guarantees, but some of these people have a wealth of knowledge – though they might frown on short-term trading in speculative stocks.

### *Day trading*

They will not fancy it much if you wander in and start talking about day trading. This American idea of buying in the morning, selling again within hours or minutes, and leaving at the end of the day with a level book, is not too sensible for UK investors. There are days when you can get lucky, buy in the morning and clinch a fat profit in the afternoon. There are always lucky flukes, or even some well-judged exceptions.

But they are few and far between for most of us, unless we are stockbrokers, in touch with the action all day, and not lumbered with paying dealing commission.

By and large, though, specific day trading is not a good idea in the UK.

Much though I love short term share gambling, that is much too risky. The trading expenses are too high here, and the bid-offer spread is generally too great. And there are certain specific rules which favour small investors in the US which do not apply to our trading system.

### *Advisory service*

However you trade, please give serious thought to spending a few pounds more and signing up for a broker with an advisory service. Most will shudder at the notion of outright share gambling, but it is always best to have a sounding board of some sort. The opportunity of testing your ideas, getting some sort of feedback, is invaluable. The bigger firms will have some sort of newsletter, with their ideas. They might allow you access to the advice of some of their analysts, and they will be more disposed to sending you written information, if you are not on the internet.

### *Execution-only broking*

It might cost £5 or £10 more a trade to take an advisory service instead of an execution-only deal. Remember, though, that a difference of 1p in the price for 10,000 shares is worth £100. A good broker could save you in dealing skills far more than you will save from cheaper commissions with a broking service where you simply phone and place an order with a clerk.

Take extra care with the very cheapest deals. Those which involve written instructions, sent by post, are too slow to take seriously in these fast-moving markets. Beware, too, of those who offer low rates because they gather orders through the day, and trade them in bulk two or three times a day. That does save costs, but when prices are moving, could be a false economy.

### *Paperwork*

Any broker these days will require you to complete long agreement forms giving what you might consider impertinent details of your finances. Sadly, that is required by the various regulators. These days, they are convinced everyone might be a big-time Columbian drug smuggler, laundering money. Be sure to specify on your form that you are a high-risk investor. Otherwise some jobs-worth will decide that you cannot trade in and out of smaller stocks.

Direct on-line trading, where you place your orders over the internet, does little to cut this paperwork. I have no direct experience of how well it works – except to know that there are complaints by the thousand when the action really gets going, and people cannot get through to trade. So when you most need it, the system tends to fail you.

That problem is not confined to net-trading, unfortunately. In the busiest times, when share prices are moving most quickly, there can be delays in executing trades. Brokers are overwhelmed, and so are market-makers. And, no matter what the pretence, they do not answer phones when they wish to duck dealing. Unless you have developed a good relationship with a reliable, accessible broker, delays could cost you a fortune if the market cracks.

### Settlement – T25 and so on

Nowadays, the settlement system has become more complicated. In theory, most trades are meant to be done for T 5. T is transaction day, and the five means that the account should be settled – you pay or get paid – five days later. That is too fast for most people. Most trades are done for T 10, offering a more relaxed ten day settlement.

The maximum allowed is T 25. This could allow you to buy one day, sell again a few days later at a profit, and simply take a cheque for your winnings after 25 days – or send one to cover your losses. It used to be routine under the previous account system for gamblers to buy and sell within a two week period in this fashion. It can be done for T 25. Talk to your broker about it. In theory, you might be charged a little extra to deal T 25, but in practice there is often little difference.

### Share certificates

In recent years, there has been a push towards abolishing share certificates in an effort to speed up the system. In truth, they are a nuisance. You need to keep them somewhere safe, and must send them to your broker promptly in time to cope with the new settlement system. So if you deal T 5, you are supposed to send the certificate in within five days. Now there are fines for those who do not, so any delay could cost you extra, mounting by the day.

### *Nominee accounts*

We are rapidly moving towards a so-called paperless system, under which investors do not receive share certificates, but hold their shares through a nominee account with their broker. In some ways, this is much more convenient. You do not have to bother about finding and posting the certificate after any deal, and there is no worry about fines for late delivery.

In practice, however, the nominee account works against the private investor. In most cases, it means that the investor does not appear on the company share register, and is not sent any documents – not even dividend cheques. The dividend cheques are sent to the broker's nominee account. He sends them on, or credits the account.

That is no great problem. Where the system falls down is that unless clients specifically request it, they are not sent copies of rights issue documents, reports and accounts, or anything else. And they are not strictly entitled to attend company meetings, or to speak and vote at them. The link with the company is broken. Personal Equity Plan and Individual Savings Account shares are shunted into nominee accounts.

Some brokers will help you reclaim all of your rights, if they are asked. Most charge for doing so. Some charge quite a lot. It is nonsense, of course, that investors are treated this way. Though successive Governments have clattered on about shareholder democracy when it has suited them – when they have had a privatisation issue to sell – they have knowingly and hypocritically connived at allowing the Bank of England and the Stock Exchange to erect this barrier to shareholder democracy.

You can ask to receive share certificates and to appear on the share register. Most – not all – brokers offer the option. Some charge extra for it.

Sad to say, no-one seems to want to do anything about it, in spite of a Department of Trade investigation into such things. It is yet another reason why the internet makes sense. It lets you get to the information your company may not be getting through to you.

### *Hunting information*

Keeping in touch is crucial. There is no point in pretending that this book can give you a proper survey of where to go, and what you will find on the internet. I have not spotted more than a small number of the relevant sites. And I have not had time to see how well all parts of the ones I know work. Ironically, you have to go an old-fashioned printed source for that sort of thing. The Investors Chronicle keeps pretty well abreast of things, and will give you a good idea of what is about, though there are several web sites which list other useful sites, once you start surfing the net.

### *General internet info*

There are several useful general news services on the net, free of charge. Among those worth investigating is www.ukinvest.com, which is part of the Freeserve offering. You do not have to subscribe to Freeserve to get to it. There is a growing tally of market reports, news, and comments, plus access to individual share prices. It carries several columnists, and at the time of writing, I contribute a weekly investment column.

The www.Hemscott.com site also has a variety of excellent features, many of them free, others carrying a subscription. It is also worth looking at www.moneyworld.co.uk, and www.citywire.co.uk. Be careful to use the co.uk appendages on the last two. Though dot com tends to be the more universal, international tag, if you put it on the end of the moneyworld tag, you reach a totally unconnected porn site, while citywire.com is an American estate agent.

Several newspapers and magazines have sites. Their value varies, but you should take a look. Much of the stuff from the Daily Mail and Evening Standard, including many of my Mail share tipping columns, is on www.thisismoney.co.uk. The www.ft.com site looks rather messy and confusing in contrast to the parent paper, The Financial Times. The Daily Telegraph is on www.telegraph.co.uk, and the Guardian on www.newsunlimited.co.uk. Do not miss the Investors Chronicle on www.investorschronicle.co.uk.

You might also like to visit my own site, www.michaelwalters.com. This is something I have been offering since April 1999, free of charge, in my own time and at my own expense. On Friday evening in most weeks, I sit down and ramble on for 900 to 2,500 words about the shares I follow and such, updating my views. It started as a service to those who have followed my tips, and was meant to fill part of the gap which arises because it is impossible to keep up to date through a weekly newspaper column, though it covers more than my Mail column.

By the time you read this, it may well have been adopted by one of the exciting new internet companies. Instead of poorly presented ramblings, it should look rather smarter, and should incorporate other useful features, hopefully including a bulletin board where we can all exchange ideas. The intention is that it should remain free of charge.

### *Internet pay sites*

There are several sites which offer real time share prices, instant company announcements in full, and valuable archives covering previous company statements, charts, directors' share dealings, and so on. Though I have not used it, I suspect most of what you could want is available somewhere on the www.Hemscott.com site, including access to Company Refs, which covers recent broker forecasts. The one in use at the Daily Mail is the excellent www.etrade.co.uk. Once you get half-serious, you will find it well worth paying £10 or so a month for the ease of having all you need available at any time at the touch of a button.

Almost all of these services are linked to a dealing facility. Some brokers, of course, give access to good sites of their own as part of the dealing programme.

### *E-mail newsletters*

It is also possible to register to receive regular daily bulletins or weekly newsletters. There is one on www.ukinvest.com. Others include www.iii.co.uk, www.fool.co.uk, www.moneyworld.co.uk, and www.moneynet.com from Reuters.

### *Portfolio tracking*

Many of the internet services offer you the ability to enter a list of shares – your actual portfolio, a paper portfolio, or simply a group of shares you are trying to assess – and will provide regular prices for them. If you pay enough, you can get real time prices. Others offer prices with a 20 minute delay (typical of the Stock Exchange to make it more expensive for information providers to keep small investors in touch in real time).

Whichever you use, it is enormously helpful. In most cases, you can enter details of the number of shares you own, and your buying price, and see how the overall value of your portfolio changes through the day. Excellent.

### *Mobile phones*

I have not seen them myself, and since I frequently lose the mobile phone I have been given, may find them of limited use. But it is becoming possible to get share prices and news via the internet over a mobile phone. That could be useful at times.

### *Message boards*

Please excuse me if I am a trifle muddled here. Message boards or bulletin boards amount to the same thing, so far as I can see. They are fascinating, and a trifle dangerous.

Though the format varies, they offer a facility for any investor to post a comment about anything in the investment world, and to invite replies. Some of the postings are mildly obscene and offensive, some libellous (I normally ask the board managers to take down any which accuse me of being a crook, but accept those which call me a prat as fair comment). The range is broad. Some messages come from people who acknowledge that they are beginners, others from beginners who think they know it all, and some from highly sophisticated and experienced players who contribute ideas and information of real value.

There are a great many blatant attempts at ramping shares. So what? If you have bought shares and think you know something good which might send them higher, why not spread the word? There is a lesser degree of deliberate misinformation. From time to time, there are accounts of company conferences, and of replies which company directors have given to letters or phone calls. These can be invaluable.

It is all marvellous fun, so long as you do not take it too seriously. After a while, you learn to distinguish the smarter contributors from the rest. Everyone uses a pen name. I admit freely that I have picked up leads to stories I have developed and printed in the Daily Mail. I have also picked up ideas for share tips, and valuable information about shares. But it is important not to trust everything.

So far, I have only found a small number of message boards, and have not had the time to investigate them all. Most fun and most erratic is the Hemmington Scott Information Exchange. The Moneyworld Bulletin Board is also good. Perhaps the best-informed is on etrade. Others swear by the Motley Fool on www.fool.co.uk. The Motley Fool has sites which provide a great deal of information. Some give it high praise. It irritates me because it has a smug, self-satisfied air, and is rather difficult to navigate, using cute little names rather than labelling the contents clearly.

By the time you read this, the bulletin board attached to my www.michaelwalters.com site should be up and running. Hope you like it. If you don't, I'm sure you will tell me.

### *Company web sites*

An increasing proportion of companies, private or public, now have their own web sites. They vary in quality and content, some get out of date quickly, and others carry all announcements and much valuable news. It is always worth searching to see if there is a site for any company which interests you. Type in www. Then the company name, and either .com or .co.uk. That should find most of them. Or you can use any of the well-known search engines, Yahoo, AltaVista , Lycos or something. Type the company name in the search box, hit the search button, and see what comes up.

### *Conventional information sources*

Outside the internet, there is a still a wide range of information sources to help the investor. The financial press comes first. It may fall far short of perfect, but does try to cover the most interesting company developments. The Financial Times gives the most complete service, though sadly no longer provides a comprehensive list, and tends to neglect smaller companies. The Daily Telegraph is always useful, The Times has got much better, and The Daily Mail, The Daily Express, The Independent and The Guardian are all worth scanning. As we move into the year 2000, The Daily Mirror is having more of an impact, moving some share prices with a remarkable mix of fact and what appears to be fiction. It is great fun, but sadly the views and share tips are erratic. Ian King has recently moved in as City Editor of the Sun, and should be worth watching.

It is particularly worth checking the market report in any of the daily papers. There is no pretence that all of the gossip they report is correct, but they are invaluable for keeping in touch.

To my surprise, few newspapers have serious share tipping columns. Though I left the Mail in October 1998, my tipping column still appears on most Saturdays. The Sunday Times has the excellent Paul Kavanagh, a stockbroker, each week, though it appears to be nudging him ever more into the margin. Edmond Jackson is worth following in The Sunday Telegraph. Both The Sunday Telegraph and The Sunday Times have sections with brief share comments which can make interesting reading.

The Investors Chronicle is highly recommended for all investors. The share tips and price verdicts are erratic in quality, but there is simply so much information in the IC that no-one should miss it. The newest weekly is Shares magazine. It looks lively, and carries plenty to read. On the whole, the monthly investing magazines are family finance oriented, and largely irrelevant. The Economist is surprisingly useful, especially on general developments in technology and the internet.

Growth Company Investor, currently appearing every two months, is first-class, and available by subscription from 9, Harley Street, London, W1N 1DA. If you can, try to see AIM Newsletter, by subscription on credit card from 01303 230046. The Durlacher AIM Bulletin, by subscription from 4, Chiswell Street, London, EC1Y 4UP is also well worthwhile. And Hargreaves Lansdown in Bristol on 0117 900 9000 offer two or three useful small company newsletters at modest rates. Contact

01303 230047 to try The Small Cap Review.

### *Tip sheets*

Best of the tip sheets is Techinvest, based in Dublin. Tom Winnifrith's Red Hot Penny Shares (which gives away my book "How To Make A Killing In Penny Shares" to subscribers), Small Company ShareWatch and Quantum Leap look pretty good, and the Penny Share Guide has improved enormously under a new editorial team since January 1999. Watch the press for advertisements on all of these, and pick them up when they are offering lower-price trial subscriptions.

# TEN

## SELLING – THE REAL DEAL

Selling is the best part of all in the investment game, when you have a profit. Even if you are scrambling out with a loss, it is surprising how good it can feel. The relief of actually having made a decision, getting rid of a burden, right or wrong, can give you a real lift.

Few investment books take selling seriously enough. It seems to come as an afterthought. Maybe too many are written by boys who know the theory, but do not actually trade themselves. Anyone who has been there, watching prices by the minute, hour, week, or month will know the importance of selling. And how difficult it can be.

You probably know the old clichés – a profit is not a profit until you have sold and put it in your pocket, that sort of stuff. You may well have read something similar from me in some other place. I never tire of saying it, because I know what it means. I have cranked up pretty tasty profits, started dreaming about what I would do with the cash, and ended up sick as a soccer fan because I was still holding on when the shares tumbled and the profit vanished.

It is not easy, selling successfully. You do grow attached to shares, and tend to cling on to winners, telling yourself there is more to come. And it is hard to sell at a loss. You invested such emotion in this particular share, so convinced yourself that it was going to go up, that you hate to admit that you were wrong. You want to hold on, to give it more of a chance to recover.

The oldest rule in the game is to run your profits and cut your losses. It is obvious, really, yet so many investors ignore it. They do exactly the opposite. Because they grow emotionally attached to shares, they sell winners to help finance their losers. I know. I have done it – but not for many years.

You have to have a system. It is essential that you impose some sort of selling discipline on yourself, otherwise you will duck and dive, and dodge out of selling shares – cutting losses or taking profits – when you should.

### *Stop loss system*

For more than thirty years, I have been advocating a stop loss system. It is not infallible, but it is easy to understand and operate. And it works pretty well. Over the past ten years, I have noticed that more UK tipsters have been backing it. But it is a universal system. Read either of the "Market Wizards" books by Jack Schwager about the methods of big-time American share, commodity and futures traders, and you will see many of them swear by some variation of it.

Whenever you buy a share, set yourself a price at which you will sell if it should fall. Set that stop loss at whatever margin below the buying price that you consider suitable. As a rough guide, set it at perhaps 15pc to 25pc below the buying price – 20pc is a fair average.

If things go wrong, and your new buy falls to the stop loss price, have no hesitation – sell. So if you bought at 100p, set a stop loss at 80p, and sell if it falls that far. If it rises, move the stop loss up behind the price, penny for penny. So at 110p, the stop loss is 90p. At 130p, it is 110p. At 180p, it is 160p. And so on.

That has a double virtue. If saves you from making too large a loss, and it also ensures that you take part of your profit while it is there. You never get out at the top – only lucky investors do that – but you get out reasonably near the top. You never end up wondering why you did not sell while you had a decent profit.

The system makes it easy. No nail-biting over whether you should sell. No emotional attachment. You simply go ahead and do it.

Still better, it ensures that you do run your profits. Instead of worrying about snatching a quick turn, you sit behind a rising share price for as long as it goes up. You make the most of a good thing.

Do not cheat. Almost the only inviolable rule is that you should not reduce your stop loss. Think about it. If your share does fall through the stop loss, the market is almost certainly telling you that you have made a mistake, that you bought the wrong share at the wrong price. Someone almost certainly knows better than you that there is trouble ahead. That is the message behind the price fall.

### *Play the percentages*

It is easy to modify the system as you think fit. You do not have to choose a 20pc loss margin every time. It can be 10pc. It could be 50pc – perhaps it should if you are playing in a penny share where any move is proportionately very large. You can ease off once you are nicely ahead – but only once you are nicely ahead. If your 100p share goes to 200p, you might want to give it a little more lee-way. At that point, you might decide to re-set your stop loss 30p below the price.

In fact, you might have started to play it a little differently from the beginning. Though it is a shade more complicated, you might have decided to sell on a set percentage fall. Thus the 80p stop loss on a share bought at 100p would have been 20pc. Perhaps when the price reaches 200p, and the 20pc stop loss is at 160p, you might like to reduce it to a 15pc stop loss (at 170p). Or widen it to 25pc (at 150p).

You can incorporate almost any variation you like, once you are comfortably on the winning side.

### *Doing it daily*

Given the instant access opened up by the internet, it is possible to track prices by the minute. Or to pick them up on screen through your mobile phone. You may well not wish to track prices that closely. By and large, I favour using daily closing prices as a stop loss measure, though you can suit yourself.

It is dangerous to leave too great an interval between checking them. That leaves you vulnerable to sudden moves, and undermines the value of the system. Some brokers might operate it for you, most will not. You can use various internet-linked or pager systems to alert you when prices hit certain levels.

You might also feel more comfortable letting prices consolidate before you shift your stop loss up. Sometimes prices leap one day, slide the next. Or soon after. There is nothing wrong with watching prices consolidate at a new base, then moving your stop loss up after, say, a week.

### *Reducing the risk*

In effect, the system allows you to choose how much you want to lose. Successful investment is about keeping the losses small, multiplying the profits. If you set a stop loss at 20pc below your buying price, you have eliminated all but 20pc of the downside. That is a very significant gain. It allows you to venture much more freely into what are seen as high-risk, high-reward plays. You get the upside with only a proportion of the downside. That swings the odds massively in your favour. If you are shooting for a stock you hope might double, think what a sensible stop loss means – a downside of 20 points, versus upside of 100 points. Can't be bad.

No system is perfect. There will be times when the price fall is so fast and so sharp that your share goes through the stop loss before you can act. That is tricky. More often than not, though, it still pays to sell as soon as you can. If a share goes that badly wrong, all too often still worse news filters out as time goes by.

Perhaps more frequently, the system will prompt you to sell a good share just before the price recovers and rockets ahead. It happens. At the end of 1999, several Mail readers e-mailed congratulating me on tipping Geo Interactive Media, one of the year's top performers. They were too generous. I had tipped Geo more than once, but stop-lossed people out at a small profit when the shares began to turn south. That looked pretty shrewd for a while. I think I advised selling at around 130p. The share bottomed at 22p and ended the year at over 1560p. The happy readers had ignored my stop loss.

And in the autumn of 1999, I got it wrong again. I advised selling flat panel speaker company NXT at 425p for a modest loss. Within weeks, they had joined techMARK and announced a new alliance which sent them soaring over 1300p.

That is embarrassing, but I have to grit my teeth and accept it. The system does misfire at times. But if and when the market crash does come, or a long slide sets in, then everyone will appreciate the beauty of the system.

Every now and then, there are other problems. There are times when a share loses all of its value in an instant. It does not happen very often, maybe once or twice in a year. The stop loss fails then as well. Too bad. It is best to look upon the occasional error as the price you pay for an insurance policy – a very valuable one. In some thirty years of advocating it, I promise it makes sense more often than not.

### *Selling half*

The most popular alternative system, as distinct from crossing your fingers and hoping, suggests you should sell half of your holding whenever a share doubles. I have always been reluctant to accept this. In normal conditions – not those prevailing in the final quarter of 1999 – it is hard enough to spot a big winner. When you have one, you want to keep as much money riding on it as possible. Selling half does mean you are left with a share stake for nothing. The downside is effectively eliminated. For the small share gambler, though, especially in the year 2000, it is better to be bolder, ride your luck while it is running, stay with the winners while they are strong.

### *Aggressive investing*

Even that, though, is not always the bravest way to play. Anyone into really aggressive investing ought to ponder the arithmetic of holding a really big winner too long. If one share multiplies massively – say five, six, seven or more times (and remember there were several such stocks in 1999, and I tipped a bunch of them) – it builds real investment muscle for you. Perhaps it is a mistake to sit admiring it for too long. It may be best to release some, or all of it, and to use it elsewhere.

Take a simple example. Assume you had bought E-Capital after I tipped it (when it was still called Cambury) on October 30. Let us say you invested £1,000 and paid 5p, well above the price I tipped it at. It actually topped 35p in the next few weeks. Assume you sold it at 25p, realising £5,000. Pretty good.

Imagine, though, that you then picked up on another of my favourites (not from the Mail, but elsewhere) and put your £5,000 into Ofex-traded Knowledge Management Software. That then doubled (as it did in a couple of weeks after my tip), and you sold. You would then have turned your £1,000 into £10,000. Terrific.

Go back to E-Capital. You would have been delighted to see it touch a peak 35p before the year was out. You would have made seven times your original investment. That sounds wonderful. It would be wonderful. It could have happened. But your spectacular seven-fold gain would have meant you had turned £1,000 into £7,000. Selling with a five-bagger and then doubling in Knowledge Management would have been considerably better. Your stake would have been £10,000.

This is pretty fanciful stuff. It rarely happens that you get such sharp moves so quickly. And the chances of your picking both stocks (though I did, in print) might be considered remote. But the examples are real. They illustrate the virtues of aggressive investment. In the E-Capital case, as it happens, the shares rushed ahead to just over 35p, then fell back to just above 20p a few weeks later. Anyone following a stop loss system would probably have sold at more than 30p. That illustrates another stop loss virtue – it helps keep your money turning over, working for extra gains.

As a share tipster, choosing when to advise readers to sell exercises my mind all of the time. At the end of 1999, for example, I was wondering whether I should suggest taking profits on Durlacher. I tipped the shares at the equivalent to 92p in March. They ended the year at 1672p, an eighteen-fold gain. Though I was convinced that Durlacher shares would go higher, should I suggest selling, and shifting that rather large chunk of newly-won capital into something which might go up faster than Durlacher? After all, for Durlacher to double from that point would require a thirty six-fold rise on my first buying price. Switching the cash to something else which might merely double seems a shade easier.

## *Top-slicing*

Perhaps it made more sense to tell people to take some of the Durlacher profit, selling just a few of the shares. Top-slicing, they call it. Tough, that one. In many ways, deciding what to do with a winner is far harder than handling a loser. The logic is clear with a loser – just chop it out.

In the end, I suspect it comes down to temperament. Parting with a real big winner is not easy. You do form an undesirable emotional attachment. And do not overlook the importance of time. Holding a winner which has suddenly gone to sleep while the market is roaring away might not be too sensible. You have a big chunk of capital tied up, doing nothing. Think of the cost in lost opportunities. Think of how much you might make if you used the money to buy stocks on the move.

### *Momentum*

Remember momentum, too. A rising stock attracts other investors. It is written about more frequently. Newspapers and tipsters start looking to see what they story might be. Once the momentum gets rolling, it can carry the price beyond any sensible levels, if it is possible to make such a judgement. Once a stock loses momentum and begins to drift, the likelihood is that it will begin to slip lower as profit-takers move in. Like the shark, it must keep moving to live.

### *Tax*

And, of course, there is tax to take into account. As the end of the tax year approaches on April 5, there will be more people taking profits in order to make use of their full annual capital gains allowance. You should bear that in mind, and make your own gains tax planning. The best advice of all, of course, is to double your allowances by keeping half of your shares in your name, half in the name of your husband or wife. That way, you both get whatever allowance is going.

### *Selling freedom*

Your tax privileges may not match those of the giant pension funds and insurance companies who dominate the market, but your ability to sell swiftly and easily gives you a powerful edge. Make the most of it. The big boys have too many shares to sell easily. Private investors, if they are sensible, trade in the kind of small volumes which can be absorbed by the market without too much trouble in normal times. And private investors have no bosses to answer to, no trustees to ask what they are doing. That gives you a great advantage in flexibility and mobility. Because you buy in smaller quantities, you can play comfortably in the smaller, juicier companies outside the range of the big boys. And can concentrate on understanding them better. Make the most of it.

# *POSTSCRIPT*

In a very real sense, this book is unfinished business. I have written it amid family confusion in the break around Christmas 1999 and the dawn of the New Millennium. I am too busy keeping up with the market day to day to spend a long period working on such a project. Some parts have been hurried, and there are sections which ideally require longer research. I trust readers will forgive any shortcomings.

The great upsurge of interest in the stock market among small investors towards the end of 1999 encouraged me that a book like this might be useful. Above all, there seemed a place for something which tried to deal with the realities of share trading for small investors, and which challenged the conventional notion that buying and selling shares should be a cautious, long term enterprise, only to be undertaken after much weighty debate.

The internet explosion has also contributed massively to a change in mood, making investment information readily accessible to all, and encouraging a new sense of excitement and adventure as investors have begun to swap ideas over the net.

It would be nice to update this book on-line, adding ideas and sections as the game develops. That may not be possible, but I hope I will be able to fill some of the gaps on my www.michaelwalters.com web site as the year unfolds. This book is an incomplete guide, but I hope it helps.

Above all, I hope you have fun playing the great share game. I love it. Good luck.

Michael Walters. January 2000.